ROPIN' the DREAM

The Story of the Ken Lance Sports Arena

1964-1994

*To, Joyce -
my friend of many
years!*

old RODEO TIME!

Ruth Lance Wester

Ruth Lance Wester & June Proctor

*award Winning
Book - Press Women
of TK 2008*

ISBN: 978-0-9795767-0-6

LCCN: 2007927026

Printed in the United States by Morris Publishing
3212 East Highway 30
Kearney, NE 68847
1-800-650-7888

This book is dedicated
to the memory of

Ken's dad and roping partner,
Dea Lance

and

to the memory of
Ruth's dad and business partner
L. L. Whitlock

ACKNOWLEDGMENTS

This book has been my passion since 1996 when I first began to research material for the book. Ken and his wife, Linda, helped me collect much of the material. Laurie Speed, Stonewall, Oklahoma, kept the e-mails running back and forth helping me to locate people. Without their help, where would I have been able to start?

A special thanks is extended to all the persons June and I interviewed by phone, e-mail, snail mail, or in person, for sharing their stories and writing endorsements. This book is their story too. Ray Bingham, agent for the country western singer, facilitated contact with the stars.

The editors at the *Ada Evening News* and staff writer, Tony Pippen, were more than gracious in granting permission to review the countless rodeo articles and photos they printed through the years. Our thanks to Kelly Ray Lance, for the aerial photo of the arena taken by her deceased husband, Gary W. Ray, Sr. Photographers, Louise Hoheman and Rhonda Hulsey, were generous with their photos.

My gratitude is eternal to my computer friends, Kyle Perkins, Ron Rogers, and Amie Judd, who were just a phone call away whenever my computer broke down.

My husband, Dr. Truman Wester, has really been a jewel during my research project. He insisted, "The history needs to be told." Truman and Ken established a relationship as "husbands-in-law" and worked diligently to support our writing commitment. Truman is currently president of the Red River Writers Club, Durant, Oklahoma. He retired as President Emeritus of Grayson County College, Denison, Texas.

- Ruth Lance Wester
Denison, Texas

When Ruth and I started down this trail, we were surprised how quickly memories came to life in interviews with people who lived the story. That is what we hope we have conveyed in the book. Oral history in historical places and times. To those persons who relived their stories, we are most thankful.

I am especially grateful to Ken and Ruth for their willingness to share their story for the benefit of future generations who might have thought that rodeo enthusiasm ended with the arrival of TV and super highways. Indeed, cowboys and cowgirls traveled the super highways in powerful pickup trucks towing their horse trailers to the next rodeo. The TV cameras were waiting for them and so were the movie producers.

I appreciate the patience of my husband, Brigadier General (retired) Richard Owen Proctor, who endured many lonely hours when I drove over to Denison to spend weeks writing with Ruth. Although he was rewarded with a Willie Nelson concert and a personal interview with Red Steagall, he was glad to see our mission accomplished at last.

In addition to the persons Ruth acknowledged, I owe a special debt of thanks to my master's degree advisor, Dr. Ralph Goodwin, Ph.D., who was overseeing my thesis research at the same time that Ruth and I were writing this book. Obviously, the skills and research methods were transferable.

To Richard's and my daughters, Tanya Proctor Simmons and Sheilia Proctor Thurmon, and to our sister, Joan Rodgers, Ruth and I extend our deep appreciation for their continued support at every stage of our endeavor.

- June Proctor
Paris, Texas

List of Photos

viii.- Aerial view of Ken Lance Sports Arena - photo by
Gary W. Ray, Sr. *courtesy of his widow, Kelly Ray Lance.*

Cover photo - 1964, courtesy of the *Ada Evening News*

TABLE OF CONTENTS

Aerial View of the Ken Lance Sports Arena
Union Valley, Oklahoma.
Photo by Gary W. Ray, Sr.
Courtesy of his widow, Kelly Ray Lance

INTRODUCTION

Is It Possible to Rope a Dream?

When Oklahoma trick roper, Ken Lance, married Ruth Whitlock, he knew he had found the woman who would share his rodeo cowboy dreams. She rode into the arena in Chicago, December 1961, as the rodeo princess, and rode out with Ken to Oklahoma as his wife and business partner for the next twenty-five years.

Ruth tells their story as they roped their dream in their own backyard. In 1964 they transformed a scraggly watermelon patch into the soft dirt floor of the newly erected gleaming steel Ken Lance Sports Arena with a seating capacity of more than 5,000 persons.

From 1964 to 1993, cowboys and cowgirls sprang out of the chutes at the annual Ada rodeo held at the Ken Lance Sports Arena. They grabbed their prize money, and headed on down the trail, roping and riding all the way to the National Finals Rodeo in Oklahoma City and later in Las Vegas, Nevada.

Ruth and Ken developed lifelong friendships with the many title contenders from the dirt-poor days of the rodeo cowboy in the 1960s to the millionaire champions sponsored by big business in the 1980s and 1990s.

Many national and world champions were honored in the National Cowboys and Western Heritage Museum, Oklahoma City; the Pro Rodeo Hall of Fame, Colorado Springs, Colorado; the Professional Women's Rodeo Association Hall of Fame, Fort Worth, Texas; and regional halls of fame in many states.

However, rarely does one find mention of the contributions made by the Ken Lance Sports Arena to the history of Oklahoma rodeo. Maybe that is because no one died in Ken's arena. Maybe it is because Ken and Ruth's arena was a latecomer in the long tradition of the American rodeo cowboy.

Yet, three exciting decades of hosting the annual Ada rodeo, sanctioned by the International Rodeo Association (IRA), the Professional Rodeo Cowboys Association (PRCA) and the Women's Professional Rodeo Association (WPRA) have earned the Ken Lance Sports Arena a place in the history of cowboy culture in Oklahoma.

Rodeo historian, Gail Hughbanks Woerner, noted in her book, *Cowboy Up: The History of Bull Riding,* that national cowboy finalist, Denny Flynn, claimed that his

2

best bull ride was on a bull named O'Bar, at the Ada rodeo in 1977. Flynn scored ninety-four points.[1]

At the national finals in 1980 Flynn scored ninety points for second place to Don Gay's first place. If he had kept his calendar filled, like Don Gay did, Flynn might have still won a national championship with his total winnings. Don Gay competed many times at the Ada rodeo during the 1970s and 1980s, winning eight bull riding championships during his career.

Ruth shares stories of other champions who entered the rodeo events at the Ken Lance Sports Arena: Ty Murray, Roy Cooper, Leo Camarillo, Ernie Taylor, Bobby Berger, Butch Myers, Roy Duvall, Joel Edmondson, and Dave Brock.

Cowgirls, too, were bridging the gender gap and winning rodeo championships. Among the Girls' Rodeo Association(GRA) world champion barrel racers, who competed at the Ken Lance Sports Arena, were Jeana Day Felt, 1974; Jimmie Gibbs, 1975 and 1976; and Lynn McKenzie, 1978. Connie Combs, Comanche, Oklahoma, competed at the finals in 1975 and placed second to Jimmie Gibbs' first place, who also won first in calf roping, cinching the All-Around Cowgirl Championship.

Perhaps the most famous young Oklahoma cowgirl champion at the Ada rodeo was Sue Pirtle, from Stonewall. A teenager when she entered her first events in 1965, Sue was inducted into the Cowgirl Hall of Fame and Heritage Museum in 1981. A movie was made of her life.

Jackie Jo Perrin, Antlers, Oklahoma, won three world championships before she was eighteen years old. At the age of thirteen, she became the youngest person ever to win a world championship in barrel racing. In1979, at the age of seventeen, she won the world champion barrel racer title and the all-around cowgirl title.

Martha (Arthur) Josey was inducted into the Cowgirl Hall of Fame in 1985. She represented the United States in the Winter Olympics at Calgary, Canada, in 1987. She became the only cowgirl to go to the National Finals Rodeo in four consecutive decades.

Martha wrote to Ruth, saying, "Ken always had the interests of the cowgirls and cowboys at heart and always tried to give them the best rodeo, best prizes and money of the whole era!"[2]

At the National Rodeo Finals only the best livestock were chosen for the would-be champion riders and ropers. Sixteen-time world champion all-around cowboy, Jim Shoulders, Henryetta, Oklahoma, knew exactly what was needed and opened his own livestock production company in the 1970s. From 1980 through 1985, the Shoulders' rodeo production company supplied the livestock at the annual Ada rodeo with quality stock that was selected for the national finals.

Stock contractor, Harry Vold, Boulder, Colorado, raised bucking horses through selective breeding. His horses won second and third places in the National Finals Rodeo in 1975. Vold's bull, Panda Bear, won first place.

4

The Steiner family operation, near Bastrop, Texas, is legendary, dating back to its founder, Buck Steiner, who started out in the Wild West Shows with Buffalo Bill and Tom Mix. Steiner's grandson, Bobby, became the world champion bull rider in1973. In 1975, Bobby and his father, Tommy Steiner, provided 222 head of livestock for the Ada rodeo including seventy bucking horses and forty-seven bulls.[3]

Other stock contractors who supplied livestock to the annual Ada rodeo were Clyde Crenshaw; Jack Atkins' Texhoma Rodeo Company; Coffey Rodeo Company; Billy Minick Rodeo Company; Mike Althizer's Bad Company Rodeo Producer, Sonora, Texas; Chris Hedlund, Hedlund Rodeo Company, Montezuma, Kansas; and Sammy Andrews, Addielou, Texas.

Trick ropers performed between events. Specialty acts featured brahma bulls and dancing horses. Clowns drew laughs with trained dogs, a bear, a monkey, and an old jalopy. The bullfighter clowns, Lecile Harris, Quail Dobbs, and many others protected the cowboys by distracting the angry bull when the cowboy hit the ground.

After watching an exciting rodeo, people liked to celebrate. Ken and Ruth built a pavilion where couples could dance to the live music of country western singers. Ken could spot talent and he promptly booked feature stars at affordable rates before they became super stars commanding super fees.

Willie Nelson sang when he had short hair, and again after he became a long-haired multi-millionaire. Loretta Lynn performed seven years. Her Pow-Wow fan club gathered in Ada, Oklahoma, from1971-1973, during the week of the rodeo.

Three-time world champion steer roper, Clark McEntire, and his wife, Jackie, watched their daughters, Alice and Reba, grow up barrel racing, and their son, Pake, calf roping at the arena. But Clark and Jackie's offspring had musical talents that would serve them better.

On a moment's notice, the young Reba and guitar-strumming Pake filled in for Hank Thompson who was trapped by the weather in Nebraska. The singing McEntires, which later included younger sister, Susie, could always be depended upon when a musical emergency arose. Shortly, thereafter, Ken introduced Reba to Red Steagall.[4]

"Do you think I'll ever regret it?" she wrote on an autographed publicity photo to Ken and Ruth. "I doubt it."

Red Steagall not only opened doors for Reba McEntire, he immortalized bull rider, Freckles Brown, in song. At the National Finals Rodeo in Oklahoma City, 1967, no rider had ever been able to ride Jim Shoulders' bull, Tornado, the full eight seconds. But Freckles was still riding when the whistle blew and the crowd roared. Ken and Ruth were there.

Later, Ken invited Freckles Brown to make a guest appearance at the Ada rodeo. Brown was cheered to the music of Red Steagall singing, "Freckles Brown," as Brown entered the arena on his horse. Jim Shoulders was the stock contractor that night but Tornado had gone on to greener pastures. The famous bull was buried in 1972 at Persimmon Hill on the grounds of the National Cowboy Hall of Fame and Western Heritage Museum, Oklahoma City.

Through the years generations danced year-round at the pavilion to the live music of many other favorites such as Bob Wills, Ray Price, Conway Twitty, Porter Wagoner, Norma Jean, Tammy Wynette, Barbara Mandrell, Wanda Jackson, Johnny Rodriguez, George Jones, Moe Bandy, and world champion cowboy, Larry Mahan, who turned entertainer.

When the Ken Lance Sports Arena opened in 1964 featuring western movie star, Tim Holt, Ken had roped his dream of professional rodeo promotion. He rode it through the 1970s and the 1980s. As Ken reined in his dream in the early 1990s he again featured an old time friend and western movie star, trick roper, Montie Montana.

The greatest stars of all, however, to Ken and Ruth were their dads, Dea Lance and L. L. Whitlock, who believed in their dream and helped them to make it a reality. One day Ruth and I were thumbing through rodeo posters and faded newspaper clippings about those exciting years. Ruth commented, "You know, June, Daddy never backed a loser."

I replied, "That sounds like the title of a book."

At that moment we both knew that we must write the story of the Ken Lance Sports Arena. As we researched Ken's love of ropin' and trick ropin' which inspired his dream, the obvious title could be none other than "Ropin' the Dream." Ken and Ruth decided to dedicate the book to the memory of their dads.

Although Ruth and Ken divorced in 1986 they kept in touch with each other and their families. Ken would always be "Uncle Ken" to all Ruth's nieces and nephews.

Unfortunately, Ruth and I were fine-tuning the finished product when Ken died suddenly of pneumonia at his home on Ken Lance Road in Union Valley, September 21, 2006. It was the morning before the autumn equinox.

Consequently, the epilogue, "The End of an Era," concludes as a tribute to the man who dared to live his dream, and in the process furthered the dreams of many others.

- June Proctor

CHAPTER I.

Ropin' the Dream in the 1960s

June's story: In the summer of 1964 Ruth and I hugged each other good-by at Richard's and my home in Pasadena, Texas, and loaded our gear for the separate trails we would ride for the next twenty-seven years. However, her gear included my four children, while my gear included diapers for my overdue baby who had decided to delay her arrival.

Ken and Ruth had come to Pasadena to attend my husband's graduation from Baylor College of Medicine, in Houston, on June 13, 1964. Richard had received military orders to report to his first duty station a few days after graduation. Our house was listed for sale, the moving van was scheduled, and I wondered when and where our baby would be born.

Ruth and I had married men with a dream, and each man's dream was about to take off. My husband would be commissioned a captain in the U.S. Army Medical Corps. Ruth's husband, Ken Lance, would open the Ken Lance

9

Sports Arena, in about eight weeks, where he and Ruth would host the annual Ada rodeo in its new location.

In the meantime they had an arena to build and I had a baby to deliver. Sympathetic to my plight, they volunteered to take the four Proctor children home with them for a few days.

A tearful good-by marked the end of this stage of our lives for both families. The children were thrilled. Seven-year-old Michael and five-year-old Terry Glen, strutted in their new cowboy outfits. Four-year-old Tanya and two-year-old Ricky hobbled in their western boots. Richard and I sighed as we watched Ken's white Cadillac disappear with our happy little brood.

No. 1. Daddy and Ken with Tanya, Ricky, Terry, Mike.
Family photo.

Ruth and Ken had no idea what they were in for. One week stretched into three weeks before our family was reunited in El Paso where Richard was serving a rotating internship at William Beaumont Army Medical Center.

Ruth tells the rest of the story.

It was amazing that Ken and I managed to baby-sit four lively kids in a two-bedroom ranch house with no central air conditioning or washer and dryer. A noisy water cooler in the front room window cooled the house somewhat. Daily trips to the laundromat were squeezed in-between frequent visits to the doctor's office to treat childhood illnesses and minor injuries.

Ken worked round the clock recruiting and supervising work crews on the construction of the arena. It had only been a few weeks since we deposited the seed money Daddy loaned us to get started.

My dad, L. L. Whitlock, was a real estate broker in McAlester, Oklahoma. He hoped that one of his three daughters would join him in the real estate business some day. Daddy cautioned, however, that you had to love the business or you would hate it.

However, I wanted to see the world and so I joined the air force when I graduated from high school. A tour of duty as flight attendant on all flights overseas to North Africa was thrilling but it taught me that I did not want to make a career of the military.

11

No. 2 Airman 3rd Class Ruth Whitlock, age 18 years

After my honorable discharge from the air force, I earned a realtor's license in Florida. Then I met Ken and my world changed big time.

It wasn't long before I had to admit that I loved the thrill of promoting a rodeo more than the excitement of selling a house. My sales experience in Florida, prepared me for the role I would fulfill as a partner with Ken. In many ways, the arena was my baby and I was proud of it.

Daddy was pleased with Ken's resumé. This was no small loan and we were counting on the rodeo to make the payments. Ken's portfolio included his years as a trick roper and calf roper at rodeos from California to Canada; and winner of numerous trophies awarded for show horses he presented for the owners of the Pine Lake Horse Farm, Mount Perry, Ohio.

Ken gained retail experience as sales manager of the Rodeo Shop in McAlester where Daddy bought his western clothes to wear during the week preceding the Labor Day prison rodeo; and co-owner with his brother, George, of the Lance Brothers Saddle Shop, in Ada.

He knew a lot about publicity and networking. He joined the Cowboy Turtle Association (CTA) shortly before it changed its name in 1945 to the Rodeo Cowboys Association (RCA). For several years he wrote a monthly column, "Cowpoke Gossip from Oklahoma and Texas"in the *Hoofs and Horns*, the official publication for the International Rodeo Association (IRA).[5]

Although Daddy didn't know much about rodeos, he knew plenty about taking risks for something you were passionate about. That's what he did after World War II when he sold his rental houses and became a licensed realtor in the post-war housing boom. He was his own boss in a business he loved. Daddy knew that no one works harder than the boss. He also knew that it takes money to make money.

With a big smile, and a lot of prayer, he sent us on our way to the bank to deposit a sizable cashier's check in our dream account. So we were walking on clouds when we drove down to Texas for Richard's graduation and returned home with my niece and three young nephews.

We took the children with us to Oklahoma rodeos in the evenings. Ken entered the roping events and we tacked up Ada rodeo posters. One rodeo was at Durant, where Ken graduated from high school. His classmates called him Cowboy Ken since he dressed like a cowboy, roped like a cowboy, and even walked like a cowboy in his pointed toe boots.

One young Durant student, Bill Braudrick, was so inspired by Ken's cowboy image and trick roping act that he later held weekly ropings and an annual rodeo at his own ranch, 1958 to 1962. Ken's father, Dea, would visit with Bill's father, Richard Braudrick, while Ken competed in the ropings.

Posters, flyers, and billboards weren't our only means of advertising. We purchased a covered wagon on which to paint commercial signs. Two-year-old Dwaine, son of our friends, Bonnie and Gerald Flowers, came over to play with Ricky the day the covered wagon went to town. Since Ken parked it at Alford's Texaco Service

14

Station in Ada, where rodeo tickets were sold, he didn't need a team of mules to pull the wagon. He loaded it on a flat bed trailer and towed it with his old Ford pickup truck.

The children wanted to ride down the hill from our place in the covered wagon, pretending they were riding on a parade float. Ken drove slowly and stopped before he reached the highway. Then he helped the children to climb down and get into my Pontiac sedan to ride with me. When we unloaded the wagon at Alford's Texaco station, the kids scrambled into the wagon again and posed for pictures.

At last June phoned and announced that she had given birth to a baby girl, Sheilia René. I was so happy that I immediately plopped the kids into the bath tub and out again to dress them for the flight to El Paso a few hours later. I had kept their suitcases half packed all the time.

The kids were happy to be going home but they had their doubts about another baby sister. Nevertheless, when we arrived in El Paso, they were glad to see their mom and dad again, which made it easier for me to leave the next morning and fly back to Oklahoma.

The next few weeks flew by so quickly that day and night ran together. Ken and I made trips to more arenas to study the pros and cons of different designs. An all-steel arena would be the safest. Every spectator must have a grand view. Ken figured we needed seating for 5,000 people to make it pay. For starters, we bought the bleachers from the old Ada Rodeo Association and moved them from the fairgrounds to our location. There was something sentimental about having a piece of the old rodeo property as part of the new.

Preparing the grounds and sinking the vertical steel posts into concrete footings took longer than we expected. By July 5, not a single pipe had been welded. A parameter of 350 feet x 175 feet required a lot of welding. Ken's brother, George, and his son, Randy Lance, labored all month with Ken and the hired crews under the burning sun to construct chutes, holding pens, gates, and fences.

Only four hours before show time the last panel of corrugated sheet metal was installed behind the bleachers, to prevent people from sneaking in free. Freeloaders were always a problem.

A day or so before the grand opening, teepees sprang up outside the arena. Ken invited a group of Native American tribal dancers to set up a small village. On opening day they cooked pots of beans and stew over their campfires and demonstrated crafts such as bead stringing for the early arrivals.

Throughout the early evening the rhythmic beating of the drums and shaking of the rattles softened the sound of cars driving into the parking area. Inside the arena on Friday night, a couple of teepees provided the backdrop for eighteen costumed men who performed traditional dances. Ken joked that the rain dance might cause the skies to open and drench the crowd.

Ken himself traced his Chickasaw ancestry through the lineage of his mother, Thelma Byrd Lance, and his Cherokee heritage through his father, Dea Lance. Ken's mother was listed number 92, card 115, on the Dawes Rolls, Stonewall, Indian Territory, when Congress allocated land to individual members of the tribe.[6]

Our feature star for the 1964 rodeo was the western cowboy actor, Tim Holt, whom Ken knew personally. Tim Holt played in more than 100 movies. I probably saw most of them at the Saturday matinees in McAlester, Oklahoma, when I was a child. I never thought that one day I would meet this famous cowboy actor.

Ken met Tim Holt in McAlester when the western star walked into the Rodeo Shop, owned by Ken and his former wife, Lola June Weatherly. Tim Holt was working as an executive sales person for radio station KLPR, Oklahoma City, at that time. He drove a stagecoach for KLPR in the grand entry at the annual Oklahoma State Prison rodeo at McAlester.

Tim Holt stopped by the Rodeo Shop on Choctaw Avenue and said he needed a cowboy hat. Ken wasted no time finding just the right hat for him. Ken creased it nicely and shared his dream of producing a rodeo. Holt told him to let him know when it happened. In 1964 Ken took him up on that invitation. In the meantime Ken and Lola were divorced before I met Ken.

17

When Ken booked Tim Holt for the first rodeo in the new Ken Lance Sports Arena, Holt asked, "How much can you pay me?"

"Not much," Ken said. But, like the hero in a western movie, Holt signed on anyway, and delighted the spectators of rural Oklahoma all three nights. He visited with cowboy contestants beforehand, rode in the grand entry, and chatted with the announcer, Doug Williams, from Smithville, Oklahoma. Doug recalled those early days in a letter to me.[7]

"When you went to the Ken Lance rodeo in Ada, it was the 'The Big League' rodeo. Ken was very production-oriented. He strived to produce, and did produce, the best rodeo around. Ken was always coaching and giving you detailed insight about the sport of rodeo. He taught you how to be professional.

"For example, he gave lots of pointers about the 'Leader Board' and how important it was to update each performance–exactly what had been done and what each contestant had to do in each event. He emphasized talking with the media at the rodeo.

"Ken Lance was a great teacher in all facets of the sport and a good coach that would make you feel important and comfortable. I learned a lot from Ken and have always been appreciative and still use many of his pointers today, not only in the arena but in every day life."

The McAlester Prison Band played all three nights at the 1964 Ada rodeo, and the Rancherettes, the girls' riding group from McAlester, rode in Thursday night's grand entry along with the newly organized Pontotoc County Riding Club.

The Pontotoc County Riding Club was organized, July 22, with about twenty-five or thirty local riders. In order to attract more members before the rodeo opened, they voted to hold a queen contest among the membership. To avoid confusion with the Ada Rodeo Queen contest, which I was already managing, we agreed that the club's queen would be crowned on opening night, and the Ada rodeo queen on the final night.

Therefore, on August 6, Nancy Ballard, daughter of Bowie Ballard, Ada, was crowned Pontotoc County Riding Club Queen. Her attendants were Frances Crabtree and Sharon Shortes. On the final night, August 8, Nancy Calloway was crowned the Ada Rodeo Queen. Not even Nancy knew who had won until she heard her name called. The dedication of all the queen contestants, in making their own posters, selling tickets, and bringing in the money they collected was greatly appreciated.

Trick ropers, Jackie and Ollie Reinhart of Ocala, California, cracked the whip and spun the rope in a variety of specialty acts. Ken loved trick roping since childhood when he and his younger sister, Junie, learned to rope using a hank of their mama's clothesline rope. They performed at local rodeos until Junie fell in love and married her sweetheart, J. C. DeVaughan. In 1948 Ken headed west to perform his trick roping act solo in California and up the west coast.

19

No. 3. Junie (Lance) DeVaughan admires framed photo
of young trick ropers, Junie and Ken Lance.
Rhonda Hulsey, photograher.

During the war, many cowboys were drafted. Ken's brother, George, enlisted but Ken was too young. Ken wasn't too young, however, to join the cowboys who entertained the troops at Camp Maxey, near Paris, Texas. Trick roping for the soldiers made a lasting impression on him.

We had some well-known cowboy contestants at the 1964 rodeo. Ben Jordan, from Smithville, Oklahoma, the Inter-State Rodeo Association's All Around Cowboy in 1962, was the only cowboy to place in two events the first night at the Ada Rodeo. Jordan placed second in riding and third in bareback bronc riding. The arena was packed every night.

Looking back over the years, I rated that first rodeo as the most thrilling one for me. Excitement filled the air we breathed. When the band struck up the music for the grand opening, and the riders rode into the arena wearing their satiny bright-colored shirts and waving their hats, eager to get on with the show, our dream was born.

Our friends, our families, and our customers came together for one purpose. To bring back the best outdoor rodeo in this part of the country since before World War II when the Ada Rodeo was the second largest outdoor rodeo in the nation.

June's children bragged to their friends years later that, "We were there when history was being made and we didn't even know what a rodeo was. We just thought that

21

Uncle Ken and Aunt Ruth had the biggest playground in their back yard that we had ever seen."

I marveled that it all happened so quickly. Only a couple of years earlier, Ken said, "Ruthie, if we could build a rodeo arena on our watermelon patch, we could make a good living." At that time we were making saddle purses to sell in local western shops.

Daddy loaned us money to open a workshop in our backyard where Ken hand-tooled the leather and I applied the dye to color the background. Bob Byrd, our friend who shared Ken's love of rodeo, would drop by after work and help Ken stitch the leather and cut out more patterns.

"Ruthie," Ken said. "We could give a saddle purse to the cowgirl champions, if we had a rodeo here." It seemed like everything we did fueled Ken's dream to produce his own rodeo on his own land. He could just see that arena popping up all over the watermelon patch. So could Bob Byrd. The more they worked on saddle purses, the more they worked out details for an arena.

I guess Bob must have dreamed of being a rodeo clown because he clowned for us from 1964 through 1972. He recalled those days in an interview with me in 2006.

"In those days we didn't have cordless mikes like we do in today's rodeos," Bob said. "Two things that were an asset to any rodeo was the rodeo announcer working with the clowns and repeating what the clown said to the rodeo fans. The clowns were there to entertain the crowds and boy did we entertain them.

"Also, the clowns were expected to be bullfighters and save the cowboy from the bull when he hit the ground. One of the differences I have seen in the rodeos in our area today is that the rodeo clowns are not seen until the bull riding events. Now the clowns are called professional bull fighters."[8]

Other clowns who joined with Bob Byrd during the 1964 Ada rodeo were Raymond Teel from Ada and Gene Dumas from Springhill, Louisiana, who did a bareback bronc specialty act.

After the success of the 1964 August rodeo, it seemed like a good idea to schedule an All Girl Rodeo on Thanksgiving weekend. However, a week earlier, Ken twisted his knee while dismounting his horse. Surgery was required.

Dr. Orange Wellborn told him to stay off the knee and give it time to heal. He might as well have been talking to one of those mules in the corral. "I've got a rodeo to put on," Ken argued.

"Then get some help," Dr. Wellborn said.

Ken called Gerald Flowers and pleaded so pitifully that Gerald replied, "How can I say no to a man on crutches?"

For the next twenty-nine years Gerald helped in every way possible from taking tickets and parking cars to taking care of the featured stars before and after their appearances at the rodeo. His wife, Bonnie, worked at the dance pavilion for several years also.

Ken had another idea. He could sneak out on his crutches and the doctor would never know. He had an even better idea. The meddlesome cast reached all the way to the groin. If Ken could get a cowboy to saw off the cast from above the knee to the groin, he could ride his horse. That beat limping around on crutches.

The helpful cowboy remains anonymous but Ken was caught disobeying doctor's orders when Dr. Wellborn showed up at the house unannounced. It was hunting season and the doctor had closed his office to go deer hunting. I don't think he was surprised to find Ken hobbling on a cane as fast as he could to avoid explaining the shortened cast on his leg. The knee healed in spite of everything.

As it turned out, the crowd was small all three nights at the All Girl Rodeo, November 26-28, due to hunting season. But that didn't dampen the spirits of the contestants, nor of my dad and me.[9]

Daddy had never seen an All Girl Rodeo, so he offered to work at the concession stand. He laughed about how his Aunt Lou would have enjoyed seeing him behind the counter. When Daddy was a child, Aunt Lou ran a lunch counter in the filling station at Lehigh, Oklahoma, owned by Daddy's father, Haden Whitlock.

Aunt Lou put him to work helping make hamburgers, chili, and bacon and tomato sandwiches. But Daddy was no short order cook. He preferred to ring up sales on the cash register. I know Aunt Lou would have loved the rodeo crowd.

I was so excited about the All Girl Rodeo that I let cowgirl, Jerry Morrison, talk me into entering the calf tying event. The calf is tied to a stake. You ride your horse to a certain line, jump off the horse, and run down the rope where the calf is tied to the stake. You can either leg the calf to get him down (trip him) or flank him (shove him over) .

My name as a contestant appeared on the promotional advertisements in the *Ada Evening News* along with the names of Jerry Morrison, champion bull rider Mary Cravens, Sue Carroll, and Miss Rodeo Kansas, who entered the calf roping and bull riding events.

I could hear people cheering me on as I struggled with the calf. I believe the calf was winning, but since I was advertised as being one of the contestants, I knew that the *Ada Evening News* photographer, Lloyd Bond, would be taking my picture. It took me several minutes to leg the calf and tie three of his legs. I was never so glad when I finally threw my arms up in the air and the judge's flag came down.

I didn't win any prize money but I did have fun. Sure enough, my photo, with my arms in the air, kneeling beside the tied calf, appeared in the *Ada Evening News*. Luckily, the newspaper didn't print my time.

RUTH LANCE
ALL GIRL RODEO
NOV-1964

No. 4. Ruth Lance calf tying. Photo courtesy of *Ada Evening News,*
staff photographer, Larry Bond.

Jerry Morrison and I drove to an All Girl Rodeo in
Little Rock, Arkansas. She entered the steer un-decorating
event and I used her horse, Stormy, for the calf tying
event. The McAlester prison band and the warden were
there. Since the prison band had played for the Ada rodeo,

they all knew who I was. They expected a good show and I gave them one, but not the one I intended.

That night I braided my hair in two pigtails. I wore a tan western straw hat, orange western blouse, and purple jeans. My Acme boots were dyed orange to match my blouse. I realized later that was really a loud outfit that looked like something a clown would wear. A few minutes later, I was the clown.

When Jerry gave me Stormy to ride, I quickly mounted the horse and, at the signal, rode full speed to the rope. Grabbing the rope I ran down it towards the calf and stopped suddenly. The calf's legs were already tied. I yelled, "The calf's legs are still tied." I forfeited my chance.

That seemed like the longest walk I ever took back to Jerry's horse. Everyone was laughing. The cowboys and cowgirls, the warden, and the McAlester prison band couldn't wait to tell Ken back in Oklahoma that I was the clown of the rodeo. I still laugh about that today.

Another time, Ken and I attended an All Girl Rodeo at Sulphur, Oklahoma. Ken was one of the timers. I entered the calf tying event. This time the calf was bigger and wilder. The calf got me down and as I went down with the calf stepping all over me, I looked up at Ken in the announcer's stand and said, "Ken, I'm sorry."

Needless to say, I didn't win any money that go round, but I ended up winning $10 at another go round. I was real proud of that $10 and decided right then that I better stop while I was ahead and forget the calf tying events.

For a couple of years I was a member of the Oklahoma Barrel Racing Association and served as the point chairman at All Girl Rodeos. I hated adding my few points each month but I practiced barrel racing and gave it my best shot at jackpot barrel racing.

The last time I practiced barrel racing, my horse, Little Man, turned the barrel too quickly and I flew off. Little Man went running without me to the finish line. He just turned around and looked at me as if to say, "Ruthie, don't you know how to go over the finish line with me?" That ended my short barrel racing career and I ended up on crutches.

Ken never did trust that horse. Little Man had bucked off a world champion bareback rider before and didn't like for a man to ride him. I always walked up to Little Man, patted his ear, and said, "Little Man, this is Ruthie. Please don't buck me off." He never did.

After that I stuck with being the co-owner and partner of the Ken Lance Sports Arena, doing my various jobs at the rodeo and dance. At least my legs were not bruised anymore by hitting a barrel. My navy blue Oklahoma Barrel Racing jacket still hangs in my closet today and I wouldn't trade my barrel racing experiences or my calf tying misadventures for anything.

For the 1965 rodeo, Tim Holt recommended that Ken add a dance pavilion and hire a band of country western musicians. People wanted to dance. We poured concrete for an open-air pavilion and eventually installed a hardwood dance floor. In the beginning, however, the seating section was a dirt floor covered with sawdust. Ken ordered picnic tables and benches to be built and painted red. Nell Shaw, wife of six-time world champion steer roper, Everett Shaw, helped me load and transport more tables and benches from Stonewall.

The rodeo started at 8:00 p.m. and the dance started at 10:30 p.m. Tickets sold well for both the rodeo and the dance. For opening night we were lucky enough to book America's number one western band, Hank Thompson and his Brazos Valley Boys. Hank had sold more than twenty-five million records. Oklahoma's Lieutenant Governor, Leo Winters, came to hear Hank and his boys perform.

We didn't schedule a dance for Thursday night but the McAlester prison band played during the rodeo as they had on Wednesday night.

Oklahoma's own Wanda Jackson and the Party Timers sang Friday night. She was born at Maud, Oklahoma. When she was fifteen she sang on KPLR radio in Oklahoma City. She could play several musical instruments and played with the Hank Thompson and Merle Lindsay bands before she graduated from high school.

Wanda Jackson often appeared on the Dick Clark Show on ABC-TV. She entertained for five years on Red Foley's "Jubilee USA." Wouldn't you know that it would rain when she came to perform at the Ken Lance Sports Arena?[10]

Someone rented a building from the Jaycees in Ada. The resilient Wanda Jackson and the Party Timers drove into town followed by a long line of cars filled with dance ticket holders. Dub Scott took the tickets at the door and the dance went on as scheduled. The Jaycees were kind enough to let us sell their soft drinks. There was no ice but Gerald and Bonnie Flowers handled a lively sale of soft drinks anyway. It was quite a night.

Saturday, rain threatened again. During the rodeo, some of Ken's hired men slipped out to the pavilion and hurriedly put up a temporary roof over the bandstand platform. The roof sheltered our featured star, Mary Taylor and her band, while the customers splashed through the dances on the concrete slab.

Although we weathered the dance successfully in spite of the rain, we promised the dancers a roof over their heads before next year. We kept our promise. By the end of the year we concreted the rest of the floor and roofed the entire dance pavilion.

Our trick roper for the 1965 rodeo was George Taylor from Fort Worth, Texas. He was well known for his dog and Brahma bull acts at the Calgary Stampede in Canada, Ogden, Salt Lake City, Los Angeles Coliseum, and the Pendleton Show.

George also played the guitar. The clowns, Bob Byrd, Stonewall, Oklahoma, and Lecile Harris, Nashville,

30

Tennessee, would mimic George's song, "Big Ball in Cowtown." However, George didn't think it was so funny when Lecile accidentally stepped on George's guitar and hung it on his big feet.

Lecile Harris was a topnotch bull fighting clown. He captivated the audience with comedy acts when he wasn't dodging the bull so the cowboy could escape. Lecile wrote his own material, mostly about interesting characters from his own family in Tennessee. Sometimes I thought that even the bull was listening.

Nocona George from Fort Worth, Texas, was the barrel clown. When the bull charged, the clown scrambled into his barrel faster than a coyote disappearing into a hole in the ground. The angry bull lowered his head and butted that barrel around all he liked, but Nocona George wasn't coming out.

Hoot Gibson, Ada, Oklahoma, directed the arena activities. Someone had to be in charge behind the chutes. Clyde Crenshaw, stock producer from Foreman, Arkansas, provided quality stock for the contestants to rope or ride. Cowboys wouldn't accept the stock whose number they drew, if they didn't think he was good enough to score points for them in their ride. Official judges rated the performance of the stock as well as the cowboy for his total score.

In addition to barrel racing, we added the cowgirl's wild cow riding event. A photo of cowgirl, Sue Canal, Mansfield, Texas, successfully riding a bucking cow,

31

appeared in our souvenir rodeo program. Sue had a smile on her face and there was no way she could have posed at that exact moment for the camera. That just showed how much she loved rodeoing.

The 1965 Ada Rodeo Princess, Linda Bolen, treated her Lance saddle purse like a trophy. Her son, Victor, displays it today in his trophy room along with his sports trophies. Unfortunately I no longer own a Lance saddle purse because Ken sold mine. A woman was so disappointed that we had sold out that she pleaded to buy mine off my shoulder. It was the last one we sold since we never had time to make another one. Today, occasionally, you can still find a Lance saddle purse on the internet on E-bay.

Linda Bolen worked at the dance pavilion for twenty years and loved dancing with the stars. "I was so excited. Here this big star (Mickey Gilley) was dancing with me and I was from a small town, Stonewall, Oklahoma. I asked Conway Twitty to dance with me at a Valentine Dance and he did.

"Boy, this was the place for me to come to meet the big stars in country music. I asked Jackie McEntire (wife of three-time world champion tie-down steer roper, Clark McEntire) if I could dance one number with Clark. She said yes, he agreed, and we danced."[11]

We scheduled the Grand Ole Opry show for a concert in the arena, October 8, 1965. Immediately following the show Rocky Stone and the K-10 Ranch Hands entertained. This time we were able to advertise that if it rained, Porter Wagoner, Norma Jean, and the Wagon Masters would perform in the roofed pavilion.

Norma Jean was another Oklahoma country singer, born at Wellston. She was twelve years old when she sang on KLPR radio, Oklahoma City. In high school she sang with swing bands in Oklahoma City. We were happy to present Norma Jean with a Lance saddle purse.

In the spring of 1966 we scheduled another All Girl Rodeo on Easter weekend. Joyce Burke, a former Miss Rodeo USA, entered four events. Gay Bernard, our contract trick roper from Independence, Kansas, competed in the barrel racing event. Naturally the clowns were women, Sammie Howington from Fort Worth and Marjorie Taylor from Grapevine, Texas. However, Bob Byrd, handled the bull fighter's role.

Attendance was not as good as expected although we registered cowgirl contestants from fourteen states. It seemed that the All Girl Rodeos did not draw the large crowds, but Easter weekend was not a good time either.

Friday night, we featured entertainers, Dottie West and Conway Twitty with his band, the Lonely Blue Boys. Later, in her career Dottie West teamed up with Kenny Rogers and put out a number one hit on the *Billboard* with their album, "Every Time Two Fools Collide."

Conway Twitty switched music styles from Elvis Presley rock music to country music in the 1960s. He chose his stage name from Conway, Arkansas, and Twitty, Texas. Mary Taylor and her band played Saturday night.

The rodeo concluded on Sunday but no dance was scheduled on Easter night.

The poor showing at the All Girl Rodeo did not stop our local future cowgirl legend from entering all six events. Thirteen-year-old Sue Pirtle, from Stonewall, Oklahoma, rode her mare, Lil, in her second year on the rodeo trail. The previous year, 1965, Sue finished number four in the state junior barrel racing competition.

In 1966 she was ready to compete for the All-Around Cowgirl title by entering all six events. The champion would take home a Miley Horse Trailer and $300 in cash.

However, it was Martha Arthur (Josey) who won the horse trailer and three Lance saddle purses at the cost of a broken shoulder from falling off a bull. Even so, she was disappointed to miss out winning the bull riding event. Martha won the barrel racing, steer undecorating, and one other event to claim the All-Around Cowgirl title. In 1985 Martha was inducted into the National Cowgirl Hall of Fame.[12]

Sue Pirtle went on to hold eleven world titles. In1981 Sue was inducted into the Cowgirls Hall of Fame. A movie was made about her life as "the most versatile cowgirl in the history of women's rodeo."

Our dads were our major supporters in the day-to-day operation and the year-round planning. Not only was Ken's dad, Dea Lance, his team roping partner but Dea maintained the grounds of the arena. World champion barrel racer, Martha (Arthur) Josey, commented that "the ground was always good and the people always friendly."[13]

Jan Storey, rodeo announcer, remarked on how bright the lights were "and so was the dirt in the arena. Ken always wanted you to look sharp, be sharp, and be ready."[14]

We built a private box for Daddy, with his name on it, at the far end of the arena, where the roping and bulldogging chutes were located. During rodeo time, Glen Taylor manned the back gate, letting in the contestants at the right times and keeping out the freeloaders. After the rodeo was over, Glen would help us at the dance pavilion.

During the ropings and barrel racing jackpots, the L. L. Whitlock roofed box stand was used for the announcer and time keepers. Sometimes I had to announce and time the events myself. If I had enough help with those duties, I would run the concession next to Daddy's box stand. Fortunately, I could usually find an announcer and time keeper during the 2- and 3-day ropings, even if it wasn't always the same people each day.

We served hot dogs, chips, and chili at the concession during the ropings but some of the cowboys wanted beans and cornbread. So Mother brought over a stew pot of home-cooked beans and fresh baked cornbread that sold quickly.

She said that cooking beans and cornbread for the cowboys brought back memories of the days when she and

35

Granny operated a diner in the coal mining community of Midway, Oklahoma, before Mother and Daddy married. I had never heard that story before.

Dea Lance and Daddy played dominoes on nights when there wasn't a roping. They discussed arena business over a game of dominoes. Dea needed water to sprinkle down the arena, and Daddy saw the need for a second well. Ken was glad that he followed Daddy's advice. Sure enough the pump broke down on the first well and we quickly switched over to the second well. The show went on as usual.

I was glad that Daddy advised us to buy an ice crusher machine. It saved us a lot of money. We bought a walk-in cooler from the ice house in Stonewall and placed the ice crusher on a concrete slab in front of it.

Daddy located a house trailer in McAlester for us to park outside the arena. It served double duty as the rodeo office and the dressing room for costume changes. Later when the stars brought their own large buses and vans, they changed in their own vehicles. Eventually, we installed a couple of dressing rooms off stage in the dance pavilion.

At the ropings Daddy kept an eye on the flag that popped up when the calf left the chute but he didn't understand what had happened when the judge called out, "String broke." After hearing the judge announce several more times that the string broke, Daddy talked to Ken about it. "Ken, I have some stronger string at home I can bring to you."

36

Daddy grinned when he learned that the string was actually a breakaway cord tied around the calf's neck. When the calf crossed the distance allotted by the rules, the cord around the calf's neck released the barrier string in front of the cowboy and the clock started ticking. If a cowboy ran his horse through the string barrier before the calf released it, he was penalized. "String broke."

Like I said, Daddy knew next to nothing about rodeoing but he did know his bookkeeping. He advised us to build up our credit by taking out loans at the local banks and repaying them promptly when due. We paid Daddy annually in a lump sum on Monday morning after the August rodeo. Therefore we always had a flow of money to keep us moving and making improvements before the big event of the next year's Ada rodeo.

In 1966 Tim Holt recommended his good friend, western cowboy movie star, Tex Ritter. Tex claimed he couldn't remember the title of any movie in which he starred in the 1930s and 1940s. Maybe that was because he was having too much fun strumming his guitar and singing with the Grand Ole Opry in Nashville, Tennessee.

Leroy Van Dyke entertained opening night, August 2. Tex Ritter was featured on August 3. We were lucky enough to book Hank Thompson again, August 4. On Friday, Bob Wills sang his famous "San Antonio Rose," and the final night Ray Frushay was the star.

Five nights meant more specialty acts and more clowns. Mark Smith, from Little Rock, Arkansas, joined Nocona George from Nocona, Texas, Bob Byrd, who had moved from Stonewall, Oklahoma, to Whitesboro, Texas, and Gene Dumas, from Springfield, Louisiana.

We were glad to have our arena selected for the finals of the Miss Rodeo of Oklahoma. The winner would represent our state in January, 1967, in the Miss Rodeo USA contest in Memphis.

The year, 1966, was another great year for the rodeo and the weekly dances. Ken and I felt like old hands producing a rodeo and staging dances from start to finish. We were the owners and promoters, and everything depended on how many irons we could keep in the fire without getting burned or dropping them.

My sister, June, and her family missed the 1967 annual Ada rodeo. Her husband, Richard, had completed his pediatric residency at Fitzsimmons Army Hospital, Aurora, Colorado, and was ordered to the U.S. Army Hospital, Kagnew Station, Ethiopia.

June was six months pregnant and managed to convince her doctor to allow her and the five children to accompany Richard. They spent a couple of weeks in Oklahoma before boarding a plane in Oklahoma City for New York City where they would depart for Ethiopia. I cried all the way home from the airport.

"They aren't gone forever," Ken said. "We'll see them again in two years." He was probably thinking that at least we wouldn't be babysitting a houseful of kids at rodeo time like we did with June's four kids in 1964.

We scheduled Hank Thompson, Conway Twitty, Ray Frushay, Loretta Lynn, and Willie Nelson for the rodeo and dance. This was truly the early days of the rising stars in country music. Ken met Willie Nelson when Willie played with Ray Price's band. Willie was planning to get together his own band and Ken promised that, when he did, Ken would book Willie for the rodeo and dances.

Willie liked to calf rope. Ken wrote into Willie's contract, "You are invited to get there early and practice calf roping. Our horses and calves are available for your use."[15]

No. 5 Willie Nelson ropes one of Ken's calves.
Photo by Ruth Lance.

39

Miss Rodeo USA, Sandra Polovkas, from Grapevine, Texas, appeared every night. Our faithful clown, Bob Byrd, was joined by clowns, Harold Chancellor, from Fort Worth and W.A. Neally, from Baton Rouge, Louisiana.

In 1968 we established the rodeo headquarters at the Trails Motel, Ada, as usual. Contestants paid their entry fees in person at the motel or by phone. Otherwise they paid upon their arrival at the gate.

At last we had a single-line phone instead of the four-party line we were on when we opened the arena in 1964. Can you imagine running a business like that? Our ring was four short rings. It drove us crazy and everyone else on our party line.

Loretta Lynn returned for the second year and played two nights. George Jones and the Jones boys, David Houston, and Norma Jean completed our list of entertainers. The McAlester prison band played, Saturday night, at the rodeo but not at the dance.

Every year we added something more to the attractions. We added cowgirl steer riding and awarded a sterling silver belt buckle to the winner. The International Rodeo Association sanctioned team ropers at this rodeo. George Taylor returned as our trick roper specialty act.

Lecile Harris, rodeo clown from Collierville, Tennessee, said that coming to the Ada rodeo was like a homecoming. He saw old friends and he didn't have to work through a committee, just Ken and Ruthie. Lecile Harris, Loretta Lynn, and rodeo announcer, Bruce Lehrke, were friends back in Tennessee.

"I always liked to see Ruthie," he told my sister, June. Lecile could make me laugh when I was running around worrying about a million details. Of course, Lecile could make anyone laugh. That's why we hired him.

In 1969, the five-night rodeo featured Billy Walker, Claude Gray, Loretta Lynn, Jim Ed Brown, and Johnny Bush. Loretta Lynn was rated the number one country western and female vocalist. We were very proud of her.

Ken always drove the tractor that towed the flat bed trailer with the band and entertainers on it into the arena. He wanted the people who couldn't afford to buy tickets for the dance to be able to hear the stars perform a few numbers anyway. For those who could afford to buy dance tickets, he hoped they would encourage their friends to buy tickets also.

Ken didn't trust anyone but himself to drive that tractor towing his precious cargo. He circled the arena, giving the audience a close-up look at the entertainers, then turned the trailer around in front of the announcer's stand.

One night, however, Ken had some difficulty positioning the trailer and was relieved when he got it into place finally. That is, until Jim Ed Brown called out to

41

him,"Ken, you have us facing the announcer's stand instead of the crowd."

Everyone was laughing and Lecile Harris, the clown, seized the moment. He ran out into the middle of the arena teasing Ken as though it were all a prearranged act. The rodeo announcer, Danny Sheridan, from Monroe, Louisiana, went along with the joke. The band played and the crowd clapped for Ken when he finally succeeded. Maybe he should have joined the rest of the clowns, Bob Byrd and Larry Menchey, that evening.

The Texhoma Rodeo Company, the I.R.A. (International Rodeo Association) producer of the year, provided the stock. Our specialty act was the popular George Taylor. Miss Rodeo USA, Donna McLaughlin, and Miss Ford Country appeared in the arena every night. Everything went as scheduled the rest of the week.

When the last people at Saturday night's dance left the pavilion in the early morning hours, Ken and I thought we would sleep a month. It had been a highly successful rodeo and we had a lot of paperwork to do to finish off the books. But that could wait. We were exhausted.

The phone rang. We didn't have caller ID or Call Waiting in those days so we always answered the phone, day or night. "Martha June?" I could hardly believe it was my sister's voice. She was calling collect from New Orleans, of all places.

We had received a letter from her before they left Ethiopia the previous week coming home to the states.

She wrote that they intended to visit friends in Germany before arriving in New York. However, there had been a change in plans.

She explained that Terry Glen, their ten-year-old son, had tumbled down a hillside in Heidelberg, suffered internal injuries, and broke his wrist. Richard stayed behind with him in Germany until Terry Glen was able to make the long flight home.

"Why are you in New Orleans?" I asked. Their airline tickets were for New Orleans because the army had assigned Richard for one year to earn a master's degree in public health and tropical medicine at Tulane School of Public Health and Tropical Medicine. They were staying with an army family until they could make other arrangements.

"Will you come get us?" June pleaded.

Suddenly we were awake. This was no dream. Soon we were on our way in our red Cadillac with energy we didn't know we had. Many hours later we arrived in New Orleans. You never saw so much hugging and squealing and jumping up and down as the boys and Tanya hollered, "Aunt Ruth, Uncle Ken, we knew you would come."

I couldn't get over how they had grown. Five-year-old Sheilia and little brother Roger shyly waited their turn for hugs and kisses. The children loved the toys we bought along the way and June couldn't wait to change into the new red pantsuit I brought for her. Their luggage had gone to Tulsa, Oklahoma, and June was grateful for a change of clothes, stylish clothes, at that.

The long drive home gave us time to get acquainted with our youngest nephew, Roger, who was now twenty-one months old. Roger's big brown eyes would stare at me, shift to his mom, and back to me again. June and I looked so much alike it must have been a bit confusing to him at first.

It didn't take him long, however, to figure it out. I loved to hear him say, "Aunt Ruth," in his sweet voice. Roger looked a lot like his oldest brother, Michael. I felt like I had always known this little guy.

It had been a very good year for us, the summer of 1969, and everyone anticipated that 1970 would be even better. We were already planning added attractions to thrill the crowds. The Proctor children were counting on it. But there would be many challenges we did not anticipate.

CHAPTER II.

Thrilling the Crowds in the 1970s

In 1970 we entered our seventh year of the rodeo business at the Ken Lance Sports Arena. No longer was it just Ken's and my dream but it was a rung on the ladder of success for many cowboys and cowgirls riding their own dreams.

As a major IRA-sanctioned rodeo, its winners would go on to compete throughout the west, hoping to ride their winnings all the way up to the world championship titles. Among the 526 contestants that year were some of our local cowboys including champion bull rider, Morris Wainscott; calf roper, Bob Reynolds; and team ropers, Jim Rutherford and his son, Rick.

Country music entertainers were also climbing the music charts to the big time. In the 1970s we could still book them at affordable rates for one or two nights at the weekly dances throughout the year and for the annual rodeo in August. Foremost among them was Loretta Lynn whose Fan Club Pow-Wow gathered in Ada in 1970, 1971, and 1972.

One time Loretta and her husband, Mooney, brought their twin daughters, Patsy Eileen and Peggy Jean, with them. Ken recruited his teenage niece, Sandi Lance, to baby-sit the children at our home while Loretta sang at the dance pavilion. Mooney stayed with the children until he saw that the girls were quite happy with Sandi. Then he walked over to the pavilion to join Loretta. When the girls heard their mother's voice singing, they began to dance in their pajamas.

No. 6. Loretta Lynn wearing Sandi Sanders' white western hat while performing at dance pavilion. Family photo.

Sandi said the twins were easy to entertain. Ken had a whole wall of western boots displayed on shelves like those in a western boot shop. The twins each chose a pair of cowboy boots and tried to step into them with Sandi's help. When their tiny legs slid down into the boots, the tops reached their hips like a fisherman's waders. The sisters toddled around, fell down, giggled, and struggled to stand up and try again.

When they grew sleepy they crawled into the bottom bunk in the guest room. Each of the girls clutched her own soft blanket from home. Sandi was surprised how quickly Patsy Eileen and Peggy Jean fell asleep as they snuggled down together.

A couple of years later when Loretta Lynn saw Sandi again, she remembered her. "You baby-sat my girls," she smiled. Sandi couldn't believe that Loretta remembered her out of all the babysitters the twins must have had. But a mother never forgets a person who cares for her children, especially a devoted mother like Loretta Lynn.

Old Ferdinand the Bull came out of retirement in 1970. Actually, it was Ferdinand's modern fiber glass replacement. The Ada rodeo's first Ferdinand was made of wood. By the time the Ada rodeo moved to the Ken Lance Sports Arena, a much larger life-like bull was needed. Signs were painted on his sides advertising the Ada Rodeo, August 4-8.

The oversized bull ran on batteries and his eyes lit up at night. When Ferdinand first appeared, coming up the hill to our place, his eyes gleamed in the twilight. Ken was waiting. He ran into the dance pavilion and hollered, "Ferdinand's coming." Everyone ran out to welcome the long-awaited bull, riding on a low trailer.

"Man, is he big," someone said. Ferdinand was twelve feet tall and seventeen and a half feet long. Those fiery red eyes glowed like burning embers. You almost expected him to turn his fiery gaze upon the faces of the spectators.

In the coming weeks Ken and I paraded Ferdinand through towns wherever Ken entered the team roping events at local rodeos. Cowboys and cowgirls entered as many rodeo competitions as possible during the summer in order to pile up their prize money and winning scores. It was my job to keep an eye on Ferdinand and talk with people who stopped to inquire about our upcoming Ada rodeo.

Featured entertainers on opening night, August 5, were Jack Greene and Jeannie Seely. I liked the way Jeannie dressed as stylishly offstage as she did for her performances. Ken and I took pictures with Jeannie in our living room, before she changed into her western clothes for the rodeo and dance.

Usually during the rodeo, Gerald Flowers and Ken walked past the risers in the arena to check out the sound system. That inspection wasn't necessary, however, when Hank Thompson and his Brazos Valley Boys played, Wednesday night. At the dance Hank turned up the decibels so loud that the patrons complained their ears hurt.

I asked Hank to turn down the volume but he ignored me. After several more complaints from our patrons, I marched over to the arena to get Ken. The rodeo events were still going on. Ken hurried back with me and tried to reason with him. Hank turned down the volume but argued that he knew what pleased a crowd better than we did. After all, his music was selling over one million records a year before we held our first rodeo. Our relationship with Hank was permanently damaged as we would experience later.

Thursday, August 6, the Loretta Lynn Fan Club held its annual Pow-Wow in Ada with a big barbecue. People always came from neighboring states to meet her in person. One fan flew in from Japan every year to attend the Pow-Wow. Loretta Lynn sang at the Ada rodeo and the dance. Governor Dewey Bartlett made an appearance also. He was scheduled to come on Wednesday but he had a last minute change in plans.

Friday, August 7, Johnny Bush was featured. On Saturday, August 8, George Morgan and the Candy Kisses performed. George named his first child Candy after his number one record, "Candy Kisses."

The Ada Rodeo Queen contestants worked overtime to sell as many tickets as possible. The winner, fourteen-year-old Barbara Sue Winters, was announced opening night in 1970. She received a trophy and a special saddle. Her runners-up were Janie Brooks and Sharon Sherrell.

All the contestants rode in the grand entry each night. They were excited to meet Miss Ford Country,

Carolyn Butler, from Paul's Valley, Oklahoma, and Miss Rodeo USA, Diana Flynn, from Tulsa, Oklahoma.

Diana Flynn held an impressive record. She won over seventy-five first place trophies for quarter horse shows; ten championship belt buckles in barrel racing and flag racing events; and fifteen all-around championship trophies. Of course she received a Lance saddle purse as one of her prizes when she won the Miss Rodeo USA competition.

Diana Flynn wrote a letter of thanks to Ken and agreed to appear at the Ada rodeo during her reign. Her record of achievements was quite an inspiration to the Ada Rodeo queen contestants. One of the responsibilities of Miss Rodeo USA is to encourage young cowgirls in the local rodeo queen contests.

If a cowgirl hopes to compete in the Miss Rodeo USA queen contest she must meet the requirements of the IRA. She must be eighteen to twenty-four years old, never married, and must be skilled in horsemanship. She must understand the rodeo events and be able to explain them when interviewed since she represents the IRA.

The winner is judged on horsemanship, personality, good grooming, and how well she photographs. The contest rule book lists the moral and ethical standards for candidates. The girls themselves choose one of their competitors for the Miss Congeniality award.

Jan Storey, IRA rodeo announcer, from Haworth, Oklahoma, informed the spectators about what was happening as it happened. Storey recalled that, "Ken set his watch with whoever was announcing. That way the announcer didn't have to check to see if it was time or if they were ready."

"Everything flowed like clockwork. For example, when the singing star left the arena, at the out gate, the timed event gates would open on the other end of the arena. A green light would signify that all was good and a red light would signify a broken barrier."[16]

Jack Atkins, owner of the Texhoma Rodeo Company, provided the stock. They raised some really tough bulls. Cowboys managed to stay on only four of fifty-one bulls the previous year. The clowns were mighty busy protecting those cowboys. I bet the barrel clown was still rolling in his sleep.

In 1970 rodeo clown, Lecile Harrison, was president of the IRA. He managed to take time out from his presidential duties to do his comic clown act at the Ada rodeo with Bob Byrd. Other clowns who worked that year were Larry Menchey from Denison, Texas; Bobby Gill from Cleburne, Texas; and Bobby Ruiz from Dixie, Georgia. Our trick rider was Skeeter Ruiz.

Tickets sold for $1.75 to adults and $1.00 for children six years or older. Box seats sold for $3.00 There were more than 526 contestants in six events competing for $12,500 in prize money. This was quite an increase since 1969 when 396 contestants competed for $11,500.

In addition to the Saturday night dances held year round, occasional ropings were held. On October 24 and 25, the Jackpot Dally Team Roping was held. Admission was free but the entry fees for a team of contestants was ten steers for $125. Each team roped five steers on

Saturday and five steers on Sunday. A cowboy could enter more than five times but he had to change partners or change ends with his partner.

At 9:00 p.m. each night at the Jackpot Dally, for a small cover charge patrons could dance to the music of a well-known western band in the pavilion. It seemed like people were never too tired to dance when the band started playing.

We always paid the band leader immediately after the dance. One hot summer night Ken stashed a wad of bills in his boots to pay the Country Lancers while he ran from here to there getting other things done. When he pulled the wad out of his boots it was dripping wet with sweat. The bills had to be peeled apart and fanned in the air before they could be counted. The band's leader, Larry Large, was more worried, however, that someone would knock Ken in the head for the money in his boots when he wasn't looking. Fortunately, that never happened.[17]

In 1971 Charlie Walker, best known for singing, "Don't Squeeze My Charmin'," sang Saturday, April 18. During the afternoon, Ken's father, Dea Lance, struck up a friendship with Charlie over their mutual love of roping. They spent an hour or so team roping for fun.

Not long afterwards, Dea and Ken team roped at Bixby, Oklahoma. Ken was the "header" and Dea was the "heeler." The header ropes the head of the steer and holds it by wrapping the rope around the horn of his saddle so the heeler can rope the back legs. The heeler ropes the hind legs and wraps his rope around his saddle horn also.

When the ropes are tight and the header and heeler are facing each other, the contest is over and their time is called.

Somehow Dea dropped the coil on his rope and cut off his fingers on his right hand. Ken saw what happened and yelled, "Cowboys, I need help!" The men rushed to maintain the horses and helped Ken with Dea.

Ken was shocked to see his dad's severed fingers. He wrapped a bandana around Dea's quivering, bloody hand, and rushed him to the emergency room. At the hospital, the doctor sewed three fingers back on but the little one didn't take. Dea had two fingers and two stubs left.

Dea saw Ken crying and asked, "Son, why are you crying?" Ken replied, "Dad, I just cut off your right hand." But Dea swore, "Son, I can rope left handed." And he did. He was seventy-five years old but he practiced hours at a time and was still roping and placing in his late eighties.

However, more bad luck lay ahead for Ken and me. One month before the 1971 rodeo was scheduled to open, disaster struck. In south Texas an epidemic of Venezuelan equine encephalitis (VEE) killed nearly 1500 horses and mules in July.

No human deaths were reported but 110 persons were diagnosed with the disease. Texas quarantined all livestock and banned their transportation across its borders until the epidemic was stopped. That meant that none of our Texas cowboys and cowgirls could bring their horses.

VEE is spread by the bite of infected mosquitoes. Texas launched a mosquito eradication program and no more cases have been reported in the United States since 1971. However, epidemics occurred in 1993 in Columbia and in 1995 in southern Mexico.

After consulting with our veterinarian, Dr. Leon Self, Ken drove to Atoka and talked to Bill Mills, stock contractor. Mills agreed he would furnish stock for the rescheduled rodeo. *The Ada Evening News*, July 25, 1971, announced that tickets would be honored at the Country Music Show in the arena, featuring the entertainers who would have played at the rodeo and dance: Conway Twitty, Jeannie C. Riley ("Harper Valley, PTA"), Loretta Lynn, Jim Ed Brown, and Barbara Mandrell.

Loretta Lynn's International Fan Club met in Ada at the Holiday Inn, August 5. A special representative from Kentucky presented her with a plaque in appreciation for her fund raising concerts for the benefit of the victims of a coal mine disaster in Kentucky. Out of her concern for the children of the coal miners, Loretta worked so hard that she had to be treated for exhaustion after the Kentucky fund raiser.

When the quarantine was lifted, we rescheduled the rodeo for September 14-18. The Triple H Company of Tulsa provided the stock. *The Ada Evening News* promoted the rodeo with action photos and articles. A staff photographer printed a large picture of Roman rider Zoe Ann Henry, from Gainesville, Texas, riding astride her team of horses.

It was amazing to watch her grip the reins and ride, standing with one foot firmly planted in each of the two saddles as her horses raced, jumped, and cleared the bar.

But Mother Nature intervened and the rodeo was doomed again. Storm clouds threatened to rain us out and attendance was low. School had started and vacation time was over. As for the workers, everyone got paid except Ken and Ruthie.

We spent the rest of the year trying to survive our losses. Ken never lost hope. By December we were looking for something really big to draw the crowds back to the rodeo the next year. Ken found the answer in the newspaper.

"Hey, Ruthie," he said. "The zoo in Gainesville is selling a couple of buffaloes."

The buffaloes were making a comeback after their herds were nearly wiped out by the Wild West buffalo hunts of the late 1800s. Ken thought he might be able to persuade a cowboy to ride a buffalo for a few seconds.

It was a gamble. The buffalo symbolized the survival instinct. We were clinging to the survival instinct ourselves since the VEE epidemic, and so would the cowboys who dared to ride that beast.

Ken contacted the zoo and made arrangements to purchase the pair of buffaloes. When the zoo's elephant van pulled in at our place, we hoped we wouldn't see a pair of elephants emerge instead. In the 1990s a circus performed in the arena and Ken allowed the producer to stake his elephants in the pasture a few days. But that's another story.

Thankfully, a couple of curly-haired buffaloes clomped down the ramp and through the chute into the pen we built especially for them. They were bigger than I expected. The bull weighed about 1400 pounds and stood six feet tall. The female was smaller. We named them Buffalo Bill and Annie Oakley.

"Merry Christmas, Ruthie. Annie Oakley is my Christmas gift to you," Ken joked.

"Merry Christmas to you, too, Ken," I laughed. "I'm glad you built that pen to hold them because they sure won't fit under the Christmas tree."

The buffaloes were a good omen for 1972.

No. 7. Ruth's five-year-old nephew, Roger Proctor proudly poses outside Buffalo Bill's pen. Family photo.

The crowds returned in 1972 when the IRA-sanctioned Ada rodeo opened on schedule, August 1-5. Our nightly entertainers were Jim Ed Brown, Mel Tillis, Loretta Lynn, David Houston, and Charlie Walker. Advance tickets sold at ten per cent discount. More than 500 contestants paid their entry fees to compete for $15,000 in prize money. The prize money totals were rising.

The buffaloes gained weight till rodeo time and were a good drawing card. A cowboy they called, John the Baptist, from Mount Pleasant, Texas, attempted to ride Buffalo Bill. If you blinked your eyes when he shot out of the chute on the back of that massive 2000-pound Buffalo Bill, you missed seeing him hang on for a few seconds.

Rodeo clowns, Lecile Harris, Larry Menchey, and Bob Byrd hung around ready to distract Buffalo Bill if John the Baptist needed them. When the rider hit the ground, the buffalo headed for the gate but suddenly caught a glimpse of the clowns. He whirled around faster than an angry bull and sent the clowns scrambling up and over the steel fence with the pounding sound of hoof beats drumming in their ears. The crowd roared. They loved it.

On another night, rodeo clown, Bob Witte, brought his brown bear along as a feature act. It was a touch-and-go situation from the moment Bob Witte drove up in Ken's new pickup truck, with the bear standing a head above the cab in the truck bed, his paws reaching out of his cage, and clawing the roof of the cab.

"Get that bear out of my truck," Ken yelled.

The horses weren't happy either. When the bear was relocated to his holding area, the smell of the bear flared the nostrils of the horses. Amid the alarming sounds of frightened horses and restless hooves, the bear had to be moved again.

Finally, the bear act was announced and Bob Witte drove into the arena with his star performer. Bob stopped the truck and opened the bear's cage. He held the bear's chain and released him from the cage, talking to him all the while.

The strange pair ambled around in the arena while Jan Storey, the rodeo announcer, commented on the remarkable seemingly affectionate relationship between trainer and beast. Then Bob raised his right arm and snapped his fingers. The bear stood up beside him, looped his paws around Bob's left arm, and gently rested his nose on Bob's shoulder. What a photo opportunity. Cameras flashed.

Other clowns who protected the cowboys in the timed events were Gary Henry from Gainesville, Texas, and Bobby Ruiz from Dixie, Georgia.

Every night's feature act was different. Roman rider Zoe Ann Henry from Gainesville, Texas, was back with her team of horses to jump the bar again. Trick roper Skeeter Ruiz mesmerized the audience with his skilled rope tricks. An Indian dance troupe performed traditional dances to the steady beat of the drums and the lyrical sound of the flute. Miss Rodeo USA, Brenda Jowers, made a guest appearance.

Weekly dances were held the year round. Jerry Duncan from Ada and his band played several years for us. The Country Lancers were our house band. Guitarist, Dusty Rhodes, hosted entertainers like Kenny Seratt at rehearsals at Dusty's home to pick and play and have a great time.

Kenny Seratt was featured at the dances during the 1970s almost once a year. One time when he pulled in with his band he noticed the name of the artist on the marquee, who had performed the previous week. He asked Ken, "How was the show last week?" Ken replied, "Well, he showed up." Kenny thought that was great because that artist didn't always show up. But Ken replied, "Well, if I had known he would show up, I wouldn't have booked him. He costs too much." They had a good laugh, watched the place fill up, and had a great time.

Kenny said that Ken always treated him and his band right. A lot of clubs didn't. He autographed his photo, "To Ken and Ruthie, Thanks and love you, Kenny Seratt."[18]

One Sunday afternoon when the Country Lancers were rehearsing, Ken told Larry Large, the band leader, that he had a brother/sister act he would like for them to hear. "Let them sing a song. See what you think." Larry agreed but he figured it was just another couple of kids who thought they could sing.

"The next afternoon they came in and Ken introduced them to us and they sang a song. . . blowing us all away. If you're wondering who they were, it was Reba,

59

Pake, and Susie McEntire." Pake and the Singing McEntires were featured, Saturday, March 2.[19]

On April 18 Charlie Walker drew a good crowd with his hit songs, "Moffitt, Oklahoma" and "Pick Me Up on Your Way Down." Of course, Charlie would be back to sing the final night of the Ada rodeo in August.

No. 8. Charlie Walker and Ruth laugh about the night's show.
Family photo.

We decorated the club for holidays. In 1972 George Morgan sang his hit song, "Candy Kisses," at our Valentine dance. Ken and I visited him and his wife later at their home in Nashville. At another dance, Johnny Paycheck and the Cashiers from Nashville sang their hits,

"Don't Take Her, She's All I've Got" and "Someone to Give My Love To."

Small bands from other places often phoned us hoping to book engagements. In between the local groups we always featured well known recording artists.

In October, 1972, Ken and I attended the annual October DJ convention in Nashville, Tennessee, where we met Kris Black, Country Music's First Lady International Promotion Director. Kris introduced us to Red Steagall who became a special friend when he performed several times at our arena during the annual Ada rodeo.

Red inscribed a photo to Ken with the words, "For my good pardner, Ken. I think the world of you." Red treated everyone in the country music business like a partner. He proved it a couple of years later when Ken introduced Reba McEntire to Red in 1974 and he opened the doors of Nashville and stardom to her in 1975. The story is legendary.

Ken's favorite inscription from Red, however, is "Ken, may our moccasins always make tracks on the same trails. Your friend, Red Steagall." Is it any wonder that Red's cowboy lyrics, poetry, and stories live on in the hearts of cowboys and cowgirls today? In 1991 Red was declared the Cowboy Poet of Texas by the Texas state legislature.[20]

December was always a big dance month. Tickets sold out quickly when we booked Barbara Mandrell and her band from the Grand Ole Opry in Nashville for December 2. Unfortunately, her bus broke down when they were leaving Las Vegas. Repairs would take several days. Her father, Irby Mandrell, who was also her manager, phoned me with the bad news. We absolutely had to find a way to get Barbara down here before the dance, Saturday night.

Ken got on the phone and told Irby that if Barbara and the band could catch a flight to Dallas, he would pick them up in his white Cadillac, towing the horse trailer to carry the band instruments. Arrangements were made and Ken was already on his way to Dallas when Barbara's husband, Ken Dudney, phoned, unaware that the problem had been solved. I was happy to report to him that the show would go on as scheduled with Barbara and her band performing.

But there was no rest for Barbara. Immediately after the dance, Ken and I drove her back to Dallas-Fort Worth airport to catch a flight to Nashville where she had a recording engagement with Hee Haw the next morning. We dropped off one of her band members in Dallas.

Her sister, Irlene, and the rest of the band stayed in a motel in Ada for a few days while the bus was being repaired in Las Vegas. Irlene spent her days with us until the bus was fully repaired and her father could drive it to Oklahoma to pick up Irlene and the band. Barbara finally traded in the old bus for a new one in the fall.

Barbara gave us an 8x10 photo of herself. She inscribed it with the words, "To Ruthie and Ken, We can't tell you how very much we enjoyed visiting with you and working in your wonderful (she underlined "wonderful") Ken Lance Sports Arena! Thank you so much for your unbeatable hospitality! Love, Barbara Mandrell."

Sadly, on September 11, 1984, Barbara's career was impacted permanently. A young driver crossed the turn lane and crashed into Barbara's car. She suffered life-threatening injuries but her son, Matt, and daughter, Jaime, recovered more quickly. Barbara published her story, *Get to the Heart: My Story*, in 1990. It was a New York Times best seller.[21]

To close out the year we had two dances on New Year's Eve weekend. Loretta Johnson and the Country Lancers played on Saturday, December 30. At that time Loretta Johnson was co-president with her sisters, Loudilla and Kay, for the Loretta Lynn Fan Club. *The Country Music News* published the thank-you letter Loudilla wrote to their editor after the Ada rodeo in August.

She said, "This was our second annual Pow-Wow and both were held at the Ken Lance Sports Arena (he is such a grand guy–and Ruth is tops, too) and up in Ada too." We appreciated their compliments.[22]

On New Year's Eve, December 31, LaVonne Dean and her All Girl Band, the Southern Belles, rang in the New Year. Free party favors stuffed with confetti were provided for the patrons to toss into the air at the strike of twelve. Ken and I cheered as confetti slid off our shoulders at midnight, marking a truly successful comeback in 1972, after our terrible loss in 1971 due to the Venezuelan equine encephalitis epidemic.

In 1973 Loretta Lynn became the first woman to be named Entertainer of the Year by the Country Music Association (CMA) and she was coming back to Ada for her third annual Loretta Lynn Fan Club Pow-Wow at rodeo time. She was featured on the cover of *Country Music News* . On an inside page she was pictured singing on stage in her long gingham dress at the Ken Lance Sports Arena. Loretta had received more CMA awards and Academy of Country Music awards than any other female. She was on her way up and in 1988 she was inducted into the Country Music Hall of Fame.

Stars are human beings who suffer the same health problems as ordinary people. When Loretta couldn't sign autographs at the time she received the award in 1973, due to three operations for benign breast nodules, she signed her initials instead. Her fans were disappointed and some were outright mad.

The Country Music News gave her a chance to tell her side of the story and hope that her fans understood, especially those who had undergone similar surgeries. She went on to praise other singing artists who had inspired her, like Ray Charles, and those who had helped her, like Ernest Tubb.[23]

Crystal Gayle, Loretta's sister, was booked for some of the Saturday night dances as the featured star and sometimes a duo with Loretta.

Opening night of the Ada Rodeo, July 31, 1973, Johnny Paycheck was the featured star. Conway Twitty sang the next night, August 1; Loretta Lynn on August 2; and Mel Tillis on August 3. On Saturday night, August 4, disk jockeys Billy Parker and Don Thomson played and sang.

Don Thomason was the popular Noon to Four, Singing DJ on radio station WBAP, Fort Worth, Texas. Billy Parker was billed as the All Night Singing DJ of radio station KVOO, Tulsa, Oklahoma.

No. 9. One of our two covered wagons advertising the rodeo. Family photo.

Billy formerly played with Ernest Tubb's band. That was how he met country music promoter Kris Black. He invited Kris to do a promotional show on his four-hour KVOO trucker's radio program. She credited Billy Parker with helping her to develop confidence in her own singing and promotional style. Kris appeared on the cover of the only bluegrass album Buck Owens ever made. It was titled, "Ruby." Billy Parker, on the other hand, credited Ken with giving him the inspiration he needed to go on with his career when he was starting out on his own.[24]

In the July 1973 issue of *Rodeo News* Sandra Garnett, Miss Rodeo USA, was pictured modeling her western attire with the Ken Lance leather saddle purse strapped on her shoulder. We appreciated the bonus advertising for our saddle purses.[25]

Another advertising boost came in 1974 when we joined the Rodeo Cowboys Association (RCA). CBS television network was filming selected rodeo sites and the Ken Lance Sports Arena was on their list. The date was set for June 3. We weren't surprised when a light rain slowed, but did not stop, the filming.

The 1950s were viewed as the golden age of rodeo, and television threatened to end that age. The RCA refused to allow their sanctioned rodeos to be televised. People would probably stay home to watch the rodeo in air-conditioned comfort rather than melt in the hot sun on bleachers at an outdoor arena. But cable and satellite TV stations were growing fast and the RCA decided they didn't want to be left behind. They reversed their decision.

Pat Hubbard, a resident of Atoka, Oklahoma, brought her palomino mares, "Yellow" and "Sunshine," to appear in the CBS filming at the arena. Dressed in her western suit and Stetson hat, standing beside her horse, Pat waved a friendly welcome to the TV audience.

Ken Chambers, who played the role of a rodeo clown, chose to ride "Sunshine." Pat loved getting phone calls from friends who called her their local TV celebrity.

In the TV commercial,"Who's the Greatest? CBS," Bonnie and Gerald Flowers' twelve-year-old son, Dwaine, rode with a group of children in a hay wagon. The announcer called out, "Who's the Greatest?" All of the children hollered, "CBS," and the camera zoomed in on their happy faces.

Ken, Susie McEntire, and I rode in the arena with other riders. The cameraman wanted to do several takes of the galloping horses but Ken finally stopped him and said the horses had had enough.

Miller's Lite Beer filmed a skit later. Ken's brother, George, was the sheriff. Jack Wiseman, an IRA all-around cowboy champion, bulldogged the steer. Bob Byrd was the rodeo clown. Six-time world champion steer roper, Everett Shaw, was the field flag man. Ken was the line judge. Everyone enjoyed a lot of laughs playing their roles.

In August, one of the five traveling Winston Electronic Scoreboards, courtesy of the R. J. Reynolds Tobacco Company, was positioned at the arena above the announcer's stand. This remarkable scoreboard was packed with eleven miles of wiring and weighed 1,000 pounds.

The Winston Championship Awards in 1974 reached $120,000. The prize money was awarded in two separate allotments during the year. In December a third allotment was distributed to the winners of the entire year.

67

The musicians at the rodeo and dance were Freddie Hart and the Heart Beats; Mel Tillis, who returned for the third year; and Johnny Rodriguez of San Antonio. My ten-year-old niece, Sheilia Proctor, patiently waited to get Johnny Rodriguez to sign her program because he was from San Antonio, and she was, too. Her father, Lt. Col. Richard Proctor, was stationed at Fort Sam Houston and the family resided in San Antonio.

Jim Ed Brown and the Kate sisters performed Friday night. Susan Raye of the Buck Owens Show performed Saturday night. The Oklahoma prison band played in the arena each night of the rodeo.

Guest appearances were made by cowboy champions, Freckles Brown, internationally known bull rider; Walt Garrison, Dallas Cowboys running back turned steer Wrestler in the off-season; and Ernie Taylor, 1973 world champion calf roper. Miss Rodeo Oklahoma, Pam Walter, from Muldrow, Oklahoma, rode in the grand entry with the other guest stars.

U.S. Congressman, Clem McSpadden, was the announcer opening night. He grew up on his Uncle Will Rogers' ranch and loved rodeoing. He took time out to serve as a U.S. Senator and U.S. Congressman, squeezing in rodeo announcing in his spare time. With his busy schedule, we could only get him two nights instead of the entire five nights in 1974. Floyd Watts, from Tulsa, announced the remaining three nights.[26]

Billy Minick, nationally known producer and stock contractor, provided the livestock. We had a winning team in all categories.

While the annual Ada rodeo was our biggest money maker each year, the New Year's Eve dance was our second largest money maker. One year we had a terrible ice storm and the ground froze. Ken called Bill Hendley, our jack-of-all-trades plumber, who always directed the parking at the rodeos. Bill and Ken worked and worked trying to slice their way through the frozen solid ground to unfreeze the water pipes.

"If we don't get the water back on, we'll have to cancel the dance," Ken moaned. The radio station was announcing cancellations throughout the county, but so far the Ken Lance Sports Arena was not on that list. As the first cars started pulling into the parking lot, Ken yelled, "Hurray! We've got running water. Come on in, folks."

It turned out to be our biggest New Year's Eve dance ever because people came from two other counties where clubs cancelled. Some people go out to party only once a year and that year they picked our place.

In 1975 about 455 contestants paid their fees and entered events for $20,255 in prize money. This was our largest prize money since our first rodeo in 1964. The Winston Scoreboard was properly installed for a second year to light up the numbers as soon as the winners of timed events were announced. Tickets sold for $3.25 for adults and $1.50 for children. Box seats cost $4.50.

Tammy Wynette was featured opening night. Normally a soft spoken person with gentle winning ways, she brought out loud applause when she sang, "Stand By Your Man." Gerald Flowers noted that Tammy's career started in the mid-1960s about the same time we started our rodeos in the Ken Lance Sports Arena. She sang ballads about country living, rather than western songs.

Hank Thompson, Billy "Crash" Craddock, Red Steagall, and Mel Tillis were booked for the following nights. We hadn't booked Hank Thompson since our quarrel in 1970 about turning down the volume at the dance. One day Hank talked to Ken and offered to perform again at the rodeo. Ken scheduled him for August 13.

On August 13, Hank's band pulled in without Hank. Not a good sign. Shortly before show time Hank phoned Ken and said he couldn't get out of Birdville, Nebraska, in time to make the rodeo. Yet his band did. We never knew why Hank didn't come with his band. We never booked him again.

Luckly, the Singing McEntires were at the rodeo that year. Ken hailed Reba and said, "Reba, get Pake and get out there on the music trailer with Hank's band. Hank isn't coming. You can do it." Although Pake had paid his entry fee in one of the events, he didn't hesitate to jump up on that trailer platform with Reba and start strumming and singing.

When Reba's mother, Jackie, saw Reba and Pake on the musicians' platform Ken was towing into the arena, she couldn't believe her eyes. "What's going on?" she asked Clark, her husband.

That night was just one in a growing sequence of opportunities that would open up to Reba in the near future. She was perched on the edge of a singing career, ready to take off to unbelievable heights.

Reba's father, Clark McEntire, suggested that Reba ask Clem McSpadden to get her an invitation to sing the Star Spangled Banner at the National Rodeo Finals, December 10, 1974, in Oklahoma City. He did and she sang all nine performances to crowds of about 10,000 rodeo fans each night.

Ken introduced Reba to Red Steagall shortly before she had to dash off to sing the National Anthem. That moment changed her life. But there was a rough row to hoe before Red could get a recording engagement for her in Nashville.

Reba's mother tells the rest of the story. "The way I remember it, Red Steagall was present at an afternoon get-together during the finals and sang a song which included the lines, 'grass about beer can high.' I'd never heard that description so I introduced myself and he told me about the people meeting at a hotel nearby to visit and sing (Justin Boot Company party at the Hilton) and for us to come by after the rodeo that night. When we got there we met Ken in the parking lot and we all went up together. As they say, 'The rest is history'."[27]

In an e-mail to me, January 4, 2006, Reba shared her memories of that night. "Red was singing with his guitar and after a while Everett Shaw, a world champion steer roper, said, 'Reba, why don't you sing Joshua?' That was a Dolly Parton song that Everett had heard me sing over at Ken's place. Red didn't know the chords and Pake was left handed and couldn't play Red's guitar and so I sang it acapella (without an accompaniment).

71

"Mama started talking to Red about him helping us three kids get a record deal in Nashville. He told her he was doing well just to keep his head above water in the music business. Mama thought it was worth a shot and never regretted asking Red.

"In January of 1975 Red called Mama and said that he didn't think he could get anywhere with all three of us kids but he'd try to take me to Nashville and see what he could get done. Eleven months later I had a recording contract with Polygram Mercury Records."[28]

Jackie was very talented herself. She taught her four children to sing harmony when they were riding to rodeos with their father, Clark. When the McEntire kids were in high school, Jackie persuaded the principal to organize the Kiowa Cowboy School Band for one semester of credit. The band won contests, and played at football games and at honky-tonks in small towns. When Susie reached junior high, she sang with Reba and Pake as the "Singing McEntires."

Jackie remembers, "Ken was especially nice to everyone, but seemed to sort of take Pake, Reba, and Susie under his wing, so to speak. I feel sure they were occasionally a nuisance, but if they were, it was never shown by Ken. He seemed always glad to see them."

"The Ada rodeo was always a good one to attend. By the time it was moved to Ken's arena from Ada, Clark had quit roping calves, but he did team rope with Everett Shaw, Pake, and many others. Alice (Jackie's oldest daughter), Pake, and Reba competed also (the girls competed in barrel racing). They always had a good time, and so did everyone else. It took a mountain of work to build it up, and everyone regretted seeing it go. The complex will go down in history as one of the important places in Oklahoma."[29]

Although Ken often hired the Singing McEntires to play at the Saturday night dances during the year, it wasn't until 1979 that Reba was actually the featured star in the arena at the rodeo and at the dance afterwards. By then her recording career was rising.

Red Steagall was featured at the Ada rodeo in 1975, 1977, 1980, and 1988. In the fall of 2005, June and I interviewed Red in Fort Worth and relived those days through the photos and clippings of the rodeos at the Ken Lance Sports Arena.

A few days later Red wrote me about those memories. "Very few producers in the history of rodeo have contributed as much to the sport and their community as has Ken Lance. When you signed a contract with him, you were assured that the presentation would be professional, the audience would appreciate your music, and that you would be treated fairly. Ken had an innate ability to know what was best for his audience. I applaud Ken for his major contribution to the world of rodeo, the community of central Oklahoma, and his commitments to his employees and friends. Ken, I treasure your friendship."[30]

Kenny Seratt played at some of the Saturday night dances in the 1970s and again in the 1980s. His first big hit was "Good Bye Comes Hard" in 1972 on the MGM label. His biggest hit was "Love and Honor" in 1975, and

"The Bitter End" made the top forty on the charts in 1983 on the MDJ label. About fifteen of Kenny Seratt's songs made the top forty. Reba McEntire once asked Kenny Seratt how to get on a record label. It didn't take her long to achieve her goal. In the 1990s Kenny Seratt was made an out-of-state honorary Okie and inducted into the Oklahoma Country and Western Hall of Fame.

The 1975 rodeo attracted cowboy contenders such as Don Gay, the 1974 world champion bull rider, and Jeana Day Felt, the 1974 GRA (Girls' Rodeo Association) world champion barrel racer. Tommy Steiner and Bobby Steiner were the stock contractors.

Tom Hadley was our rodeo announcer. Ken liked the way Tom stood out in his western tuxedo. Tom Hadley wore patent leather boots and a white hat, tuxedo pants, and a tuxedo coat when the weather wasn't too hot. He was inducted into the Rodeo Historical Society's Cowboy Hall of Fame, Oklahoma City, in 2005. None other than Clem McSpadden introduced him and presented the award. [31]

Two weeks before the 1976 rodeo, Ken roped a coyote running toward our neighbor's chickens. To his surprise the animal ran right up the rope and sank his teeth into Ken's arm. Ken wrestled that coyote loose, hogtied the animal, and tied his mouth shut.

I was afraid that the coyote had rabies. So I phoned my brother-in-law, Richard Proctor, M.D., who also held a master's degree in public health and tropical medicine. Richard told us to call the veterinarian and tell him to send the coyote's head off to be examined for rabies.

A photographer from the *Ada Evening News* took a picture of Ken with the live coyote. Ken knelt down on one knee, and laid the hogtied coyote on the ground, supporting the coyote's head with his bare hand. I couldn't believe that Ken didn't even wear leather gloves for protection.

He delivered the coyote to the veterinarian. The coyote's head was wrapped and packaged for mailing by express mail. Time was critical. Unfortunately, the package got left behind on the loading dock over the weekend. In the summer heat, the head rotted and couldn't be accurately tested for rabies.

Richard phoned the Communicable Disease Control Center in Atlanta, Georgia, and within hours the rabies vaccine was flown to Oklahoma City. Ken's doctor started him on the painful series of shots immediately.

Poor Ken. He was so sore from taking the shots. He had a miserable time riding in the grand entry at the rodeo carrying the American flag. Ken learned his lesson and never roped a coyote again.

The rodeo of 1976 was very sad for me. A few months before the rodeo Ken and I filed for divorce. I was giving up my baby. That was what I called the rodeo–my baby. It wasn't easy for me. I had put so much of my life into the business that it was very hard to leave.

Ken phoned June and Richard. They lived in San Antonio, Texas, where Richard was stationed at Fort Sam Houston. Ken asked if I could come and visit them a few days. They welcomed me with open arms. All I did was cry in the upstairs bedroom of their home. I missed my friends in Ada, Oklahoma. A few days later I flew back to Oklahoma City where my friend, Mae Littell, picked me up at the airport.

I stayed with Mae and Gene Littell and their two sons in Ada until I was able to rent a one-bedroom apartment from Ken's ex-sister-in-law, Fran Lance, for $110 a month. Fran and I always enjoyed our coffee chats and shopping sprees together.

As the rodeo drew closer, the reality hit me hard that I wasn't going to be a part of it this year. With an aching heart, I followed the newspaper articles and advertisements. About 400 contestants would compete for $22,000 to $24,000 in prize money. Again the Winston Pro Rodeo electronic scoreboard would display the winning numbers.

I read that trick riders, Janette Plunkett, from Abbott, Texas, and J. W. Stoker from Weatherford, Texas, would be performing. They were always great crowd-pleasers. Quail Dobbs, from Coahoma, Texas and Tommy Lucia, from Weatherford, Texas, would be the bull fighter clowns. The Matt Dryden Rodeo Company of Marianna, Florida, was bringing the livestock.

My heart was breaking with every line I read. Then the Sunday before the Ada Pro Rodeo began, I received a phone call from Gerald and Bonnie Flowers. They said that Ken told them to call me. They needed me to tell them how to arrange the box seats, how they were numbered, and where the section was roped off. That was always one of my many duties, because we folded up the chairs after the last night and stored them for the next year.

Bonnie asked how much merchandise to order for the dance. Ken didn't know because I always placed the orders. Everywhere Ken turned, people asked him how to do things." Ruthie always did that," he would tell them. "Call Ruthie." I always managed the rodeo queen contest, the office, advertising, and much more. Ken finally got it all covered with good help. I was glad for him.

Ken wanted me to attend the rodeo even though we had filed for divorce. On opening night I was sitting with Barbara Mandrell's father at the dance pavilion next to the band stand when Barbara kindly announced, "I want to thank Ken and Ruth for having me back again."

I wasn't even a part of it and I thought that was nice of her. I cried all during the dance and realized that I could not take another night of the rodeo as a spectator, knowing in my heart that I helped to build it where it was in 1976.

Looking at the list of celebrities Ken booked for the rest of the week–Willie Nelson, Mel Tillis, Jack Green, Jeannie Sealy, and George Jones–I felt like they were old friends. I knew that I could not live in Ada, therefore, and not be Mrs. Ken Lance. The Ken Lance Sports Arena and the rodeo were my family, my baby, my life. I must go somewhere else if I were to going to build a new life.

The next day I left Ada. I crammed all my personal belongings into a second hand car I bought, left word at the arena where Ken could find me, and headed to Tulsa. He was surprised when he heard that I had gone.

77

I got a job at Camelot Inn as a switchboard operator. Ken called me the following Monday after he returned from McAlester where he paid Daddy the annual loan payment. Mother and Daddy had not gone to the rodeo since I was no longer a part of it. Daddy and Ken had always been close and Daddy was very distressed at our separation.

Ken said that Granny, my mother's mother, had phoned him and cried. She didn't want to see us divorced either. She always looked forward to going with Mother and Daddy to the rodeo and to her visits when I would bring her over to stay a few days. When I was a child I would stay as long as two or three weeks at a time with Granny on the farm during the summer. Granny loved coming to our home.

Then Ken told me that he would take a few days off and come see me. I said, "Ken, when you come, bring the motor home to bring my things back home. If we don't have the divorce set aside, I will leave Tulsa and you will never hear from me again. In other words, we either go back together or I will plan a life separate."

I worked about two weeks at the Camelot Inn where the International Rodeo Association held their annual convention. Ken and I knew the manager, Bill Moore, and his wife, who worked the front desk. When Ken came with the motor home, we returned to Ada and had the divorce set aside. My parents, sisters, family and friends were glad we were back together. The partnership was again, Ken and Ruthie.

Immediately, I picked up the reins of my share of the responsibilities, starting with the weekly dances. I had missed hearing Willie Nelson perform at the rodeo but he would be back again to do a concert in the arena on October 22. He always drew the college crowd and football players. College student, Melinda Pierce, described how Willie's 1976 rodeo appearance thrilled her and her sisters, Leah and Nancy.

"Willie had long clean shiny hair, wore a straw hat, and, of course, a bandana. He was smiling big and serenading us with that incredibly unique voice that still brings a smile to my face, and makes my feet start moving.

"My best friend, Laura Harryman, and I managed to inch our way up to the front of the stage where Willie was performing. We did not have paper, so we did like some of the others were doing. We took off our leather belts and got his autograph."[32]

Those were the days when long hair was associated with the peaceniks and pot smokers. Therefore Ken warned Willie, when he booked him for the October 22 concert and dance, that the sheriff frowned on long hair. Willie took the hint.

Gone was the long shiny hair admired by his fans when Willie showed up. Most folks didn't recognize a shorthaired Willie Nelson until he started strumming his guitar and singing. Throughout the evening he wore caps and hats that the audience tossed his way. Then he tossed them back again and grabbed another one. What a show. Can you believe that tickets sold for only $5.50 advance and $7.50 at the gate? The show closed at midnight. Sheriff's orders.

At the 1977 annual Ada rodeo, Judy Lynn, a former Miss Idaho in the Miss America pageant, entertained with her yodeling on opening night. She was amazing. No wonder she once held the title of America's Champion Girl Yodeler. Not only her voice but also her costumes were astounding too.

I loved Judy's rhinestone-studded outfit complete with color-coordinated western hat and boots. Even her band wore costumes to match Judy's color for each performance. Judy Lynn's wardrobe consisted of about 100 outfits custom-made for her by the famous Nudie's of Hollywood, who designed western wear for all the big western movie stars.

Moe Bandy, rated the most promising male vocalist of 1977 by the Academy of Country Music, was featured the second night. The PRCA (Pro Rodeo Cowboys Association) voted him Entertainer of the Year in 1975. The third night Red Steagall and his Coleman County Cowboys performed. Red composed and sang many of his own lyrics.

The fourth night Barbara Fairchild, best known for "The Teddy Bear Song," entertained. She was nominated as the Top Female Vocalist of the Year by the Academy of Country Music in California. Barbara was only twenty-six years old but already she had made several concert tours in Europe.

Saturday night, our patrons had the best of two worlds–rodeo and entertainment–in the performances of one person, the six-time all-around world champion cowboy, Larry Mahan. He produced his first record album in 1976, "King of the Rodeo." It was released by Warner Brothers Records

Ken was the first to bring Larry Mahan, movie star and cowboy champion, to Oklahoma as an entertainer. Mahan even handed out his own business cards.

Mahan starred in the movie, "The Great American Cowboy," in 1973, which won an Oscar for the best documentary feature. The movie boosted national and international interest in the professional sport of rodeo for a while. Mahan participated in over 1200 rodeos during his ten-year rodeo career and still had the energy and the talent to make it as a cowboy entertainer.

Bruce Papon, rodeo clown from Hardner, Kansas, and Bob Romer, the National Finals Rodeo Clown from Canyon, Texas, put on hilarious acts.

Connie Combs GRA (Girls' Rodeo Association) world champion barrel racer, was also featured. Don Endsley of Nashville, Arkansas, and Jon White, San Antonio, Texas, were our announcers. The Harry Vold Rodeo Company of Fowler, Colorado, was our stock contractor. Of course the big Winston scoreboard was again installed.

Tickets sold for $3.50 advance, $4.00 at the gate. Box seats sold for $5.00. Tickets for children under twelve years of age cost $1.50 for advance, $1.75 at the gate.

81

As always, children under six were admitted free. The prize money was good at $18,000 to $20,000.

Our house band, the Country Lancers, were with us eleven years. Larry Large, band leader and drummer, Dusty Rhodes, lead guitarist, and Sid Manuel, bass guitarist, sang lively popular western tunes while Furmon Huff played the fiddle and Tom Trivitt played the steel guitar.

One Saturday night, Larry Large drove to Wilburton after the dance to be with his wife, Carol, and her relatives. Carol's grandfather had died. The next morning an Ada taxi driver appeared on her grandmother's front porch and delivered a bouquet of long stemmed red roses to Carol. The message on the card read, "Thinking of you. . . Ken and Ruth."

In an e-mail, October 25, 2006, Larry said, "I still don't know how Ken managed to find a florist on Sunday morning . The fact that he had the flowers delivered by taxi ninety miles away was overwhelming to us. Ken and Ruth always had a special place in our hearts since that Sunday."[33]

The 1978 rodeo witnessed an unexpected plane crash in the pasture adjoining the arena. Nell Shaw, wife of Everett Shaw, six times world champion cowboy, said she thought the plane was going to land on top of them.

However, pilot, Bob Brooks, Fort Worth, Texas, managed to steer the single-engine prop plane toward the vacant pasture as it lost altitude. Bob Brooks, Randy Majors, past runner-up for world champion bull rider, and two other cowboys entered their events that night and flew out the next day on another plane to a rodeo in Casper, Wyoming.

After that night, Ken told the cowboys to circle the arena before landing at the Ada airport and he would send a driver to pick them up. The next year we rented an old limousine. When the cowboys circled the arena in their small aircraft, guess who was the only one available to pick them up? Ruthie. I headed for the airport and hoped that I hadn't forgotten anything that needed to be done at the dance pavilion in my absence.

I introduced myself as Ken Lance's wife, Ruthie. The surprised saddle bronc riders threw their saddles in the back and I chauffeured them to the arena in style. Another driver took them to their plane later since I had to manage the dance.

The rest of the week I drove the limo for errands in town because I didn't have time to hunt for my car keys. When I drove through the drive-through window at the bank to make the deposits I told the surprised teller, "Don't even ask why I'm driving this limo." She laughed and shook her head.

Billy "Crash" Craddock starred opening night. The following nights Mickey Gilley, Hank Williams, Jr., and Johnny Rodriguez were featured.

Rain threatened on Friday night but it was the lightning that scared off Johnny Rodriguez at the last minute. He refused to put his band and himself at risk on the tractor-pulled platform to entertain in the arena. But he played a great performance at the indoor dance in the pavilion. On Saturday night, Larry Mahan returned for the second year.

Tom Hadley and Don Endsley shared the microphone, introducing guests and announcing the events. Harry Vold was our stock contractor. Several world champion barrel racers from the Girls Rodeo Association (GRA) made appearances as did Miss Rodeo Oklahoma, 1977-1978, Rhonda Steenberger.

Many of our local rodeo queen contestants came from Stonewall High School. On page 2 of the school annual, "The Longhorn," a photo of the Longhorn staff was pictured riding Ferdinand the Bull advertising the five-day 1978 Ada rodeo. Waving to the photographer were Ricky Kelly, Rita Wood, Paula Hayes, Anita Stokes, Steve Scott, and the editorial advisor, Mrs. June Scott.

In 1979 we shortened the rodeo to four nights but we featured two stars on opening night–Moe Bandy and the Rodeo Clowns plus Larry Mahan.

Glamorous Barbara Fairchild sang the second night, followed by Reba McEntire on Friday night with the Singing McEntires (her brother Pake and sister Susie).

Reba had come a long way since she sang the National Anthem in 1974 at the National Finals Rodeo in Oklahoma City where Ken introduced her to Red Steagall. Reba e-mailed me in 2006, "I wouldn't be doing what I'm doing today if I had not met Ken Lance."[34]

On Saturday night gospel singer, J. D. Sumner, and the Stamps appeared. J. D. had sung for twenty years with the Blackwood Brothers. The Stamps played soft rock, pop, and country western as well as gospel music. The Rock Busters band from the reformatory at Granite, Oklahoma, played opening night and the final night.

No. 10. Moe Bandy and Larry Mahan share a joke at the Ken Lance Sports Arena. Photo by Louise Hoehman.

No. 11. The Singing McEntires. Pake and Susie on stage.
Reba out front. Photo by Louise Hoehman.

Miss Rodeo Oklahoma, Leslie Krause, Ponca
City, appeared every night. Tom Hadley from Mason,
Texas, was the announcer. Our clowns were Rex Dunn,
from Burwell, Oklahoma; Roger Mawson from Fort
Smith, Arkansas, who brought the Winston scoreboard;

Johnny Tatum, from Laveen, Arizona, who did a feature act with a monkey at the 1976 National Finals Rodeo in Oklahoma City.

Ken and I were members of the International Country Music Talent Buyers Association. He was a vice president for three years. We looked forward to attending their conferences in Nashville to meet and book the most promising newcomers for the rodeo.

Cowboys in the team roping events were honored when the legendary six times world champion steer roper, Everett Shaw, came out of retirement to team rope with his grandson, Neil Worrell.

Three months later Everett underwent open heart surgery. Everything seemed to be going as well as could be expected. Nell walked down the hall with some visitors. As they were talking, the blue code alert sounded over the intercom. Nell had heard it before when she sat with Everett and always said a prayer for the patient it concerned. She had no idea that this time the alarm was sounded for Everett. In those few moments he died.[35]

The following month, December 1979, he was inducted into the Pro Rodeo Hall of Fame in Colorado Springs, Colorado. More honors followed. Everett Shaw was inducted into Oklahoma City's Rodeo Hall of Fame in 1980; the Pendleton, Oregon, Hall of Fame in 1995; the Western Heritage Hall of Fame in Cheyenne, Wyoming in 2003; and the Will Rogers Stampede Hall of Fame in Claremore, Oklahoma, in 2005.

Everett's widow, Nell Shaw, remained a lifelong friend to Ken and me. She worked every rodeo from the beginning in 1964 to the last rodeo in 1993.

The decade of the 1970s was a thrilling time for the rodeo crowds. But the world was changing in ways that would impact on all rodeo promoters in the 1980s.

Chapter III.

Thrilling the Crowds in the 1980s

The 1980s saw many changes on the national scene in rodeo. Big business contributed millions of dollars to prize money. Rodeo cowboys were viewed as professional athletes. For the first time in the sport of rodeo a cowboy champion could actually ride away from the national finals a millionaire.

Changes were in order at the Ken Lance Sports Arena too. Ken contracted with Jim Shoulders, sixteen-time world champion cowboy, to provide the livestock for the Ada rodeo. In 1962 Shoulders opened one of the first rodeo schools. He offered a five-day course in three riding events at his ranch at Henryetta, Oklahoma. Other champions were offering courses too.

In the 1970s Shoulders joined with Don Day, Mesquite, Texas, in the rodeo stock production business. Later he sold out his share of the partnership and started his own business in Oklahoma on his 5000-acre ranch.

Aside from his world championships dating back to 1949 for his first world title, Jim Shoulders, the stock

89

producer, was probably best known for raising Tornado, the toughest bull in rodeo. That bull had thrown 220 riders. Soldiers say, "Know your enemy." Freckles Brown knew Tornado. He studied that bull so well that he could anticipate his every move in the next instant. His strategy paid off.

In 1967 at the National Finals Rodeo in Oklahoma City, the crowd went wild when the whistle blew and Freckles triumphed over Tornado. Ken and I were there, shouting, stomping, clapping with the thousands of other spectators . I laughed and cried at the same time. Six-time world champion steer roper, Everett Shaw, claimed that Freckles could have been elected governor that night. Red Steagall was so inspired that he wrote a song, "Freckles Brown," commemorating the historic ride.

At the 1980 Ada rodeo, the famous Freckles needed no introduction. He simply rode into the arena to the delightful music of Red Steagall and his Coleman County Cowboys singing, "Freckles Brown." Jim Shoulders was there too. However, Tornado had gone on to greener pastures. The bull had died in 1972 and was buried on Persimmon Hill at the National Cowboy Hall of Fame in Oklahoma City.

More than 400 cowboys and cowgirls competed for $30,000 in prize money at the Ada rodeo in 1980. Only sixty rodeos were chosen nationwide for the Winston scoreboard. Again the Ada rodeo at the Ken Lance Sports Arena was one of them.

Joe Stampley and his Western Band performed Thursday. Originally from Springhill, Louisiana, Joe wrote most of his own lyrics. Country music was producing a variety of styles, called metropolitan country, middle-of-the road, and rockabilly. Joe Stampley played them all.

Gene Watson, on the other hand, sang his own style of country music with his band, the Farewell Party, on Friday night. His number one singles in the 1970s were "Where Love Begins" (1975) and "Should I Come Home or Should I Go Crazy?" (1979). Gene was born in Palestine, Texas, and raised in Paris, Texas, where he worked at an auto repair shop before he left to pursue a singing career. Gene Watson claimed that Ken was his favorite promoter.[36]

Reba McEntire and the Singing McEntires, Pake and Susie, entertained Saturday night. Although Red Steagall wasn't there to hear Reba sing because he had gone on to perform elsewhere, the rodeo audience was treated to live performances by both Red and Reba in the same week. In a letter to Ken, Reba confirmed two contracts for 1981 and congratulated him on being honored with the Rodeo Man of the Year award by the *Shortgrass Country News.*[37]

Ken was named the1980 Committee Man of the Year by the Women's Professional Rodeo Association (WPRA) for adding prize money to cowgirl events equal to that added to cowboy events. After years of pushing the equal prize money at PRCA rodeos, the WPRA prize money reached more than $1.1million in 1982.

A junior girls' barrel racing event, open to ages six to twelve, was scheduled to follow the GRA (Girls' Rodeo Association) barrel racing competition. At age thirteen the girls could compete with the WPRA contenders. In fact, Jackie Perrin, Antlers, Oklahoma, won her first world title at age thirteen. Jan Hansen won her first world title at age eighteen.

Tom Hadley, Mason, Texas, and Dr. Lynn Phillips, Fort Worth, announced the rodeo events. Quail Dobbs, Kalahoma, Texas; George Taylor, Fort Worth; and Robert Smets, San Martin, California, performed the clown acts.

In 1981 the Coors Chute Out Series featured world champion cowboy, Roy Cooper, from Durant, Oklahoma, and world champion team roper, Tea Woolman. Roy Cooper won the calf roping competition at the Ada Pro Rodeo in 1981, as he did in 1980.

If a contender beat the world champion he got a check for $1,000 and the champion received $300, win or lose. But if the world champion won, he got all the money, a total of $1,300. In 1980 only twenty-five rodeos were selected for the Coors Chute Out Series by the eight world champions. This was raised to thirty rodeos in 1981.[38]

The Nestea Top Hand Teenage Challenge, from 1979 to1982, offered a $200 scholarship to the winners in three events among four of the top high school rodeo contestants in the state at rodeos sanctioned by the PRCA and the WPRA. In 1981 Nestea added $1300 to the purse money at the Ada Pro Rodeo. The winners went to the finals at Mesquite, Texas.

The Winston Rodeo Series added the winners' scores to the overall Winston Pro Rodeo competition. Only seventy rodeos were chosen nationwide in 1980.

Seventy-three rodeos were selected in 1981 for the Winston Rodeo Series.

The dance pavilion was enlarged to accommodate over 1,000 people. A recreation area was added where riders paid to ride a mechanical bucking bull with down-turned horns so no one would be injured.

Mel Odom, a college student from East Central State Teachers College, Ada, Oklahoma, prided himself on never being thrown by the bucking bull until the machine was turned up to the top speed. Not bad for a fiction writer, not a cowboy rider. Years later Mel was inducted into the Oklahoma Professional Writers Hall of Fame with more then 132 published books to his credit.

Also in the recreation area, a fiber glass horse with a saddle and rope stood ready to be mounted by a rider who would practice roping a dummy steer. During intermission while the band and singers took a break, stick horse barrel racing was conducted on the dance floor with prizes going to the winners.

Moe Bandy and The Rodeo Clowns performed opening night. His song, "It's a Cheating Situation," won the Song of the Year Award in 1980 from the Academy of Country Music. Reba McEntire, Gene Watson, and Joe Stampley returned to entertain at the 1981 rodeo also.

Reba had just released her third album, "Feel the Fire." Gene Watson was listed in1980 as number thirteen in the best of singles. He had eight albums on the charts but he considered the one he was releasing in 1981 to be the best album of his career. Joe Stampley and his band, Country Feeling, had recorded several number one hits.

Stampley and Moe Bandy received the Vocal Duo of the Year award in 1979 from the Country Music Association in Nashville.

The trick riding team, Leon and Vicki Adams, from Stuart, Oklahoma, put on the Adams Horse and Bull Show every night. Leon rode Roman style standing on the backs of his two eight-year-old Brahma bulls, Red Cloud and Geronimo. Leon started training them when they were two years old. The bulls starred in a movie, "The Last Flight of Noah's Ark."

Leon Adams also entered the steer wrestling event. He won that event during the 1974 Ada rodeo. Leon's wife, Vicki, showcased her famous dancing horses, One Little One and Indian Two.

We always promoted the rodeo as a family event with contests for even the little ones in the calf scramble. Some of the families also helped us out wherever we needed them. Ken trained fourteen-year-old Todd Jackson to run one of the two spotlights on the arena. Sometimes spot lighters would get distracted and fail to turn the limelight on the cowboy who was doing his best to hang on for a few seconds.

Todd, however, never let that happen. Perhaps he was so attentive because 1981 was the first year that he heard Reba sing and he was really excited to be a part of the spotlight crew. Todd did such a good job that Ken assigned him the same job in 1982 and 1983.

Todd's brother, Terry Dean, and their father, Terry Jackson, cooled down Ken's horse each night after the grand entry. Joey Larson cooled down my horse. The

94

rodeo announcer would introduce, "Ken and Ruth Lance, your host and hostess tonight." We would ride in together on our horses. Ken would ride to the left side of the arena and I would ride to the right. We would meet in the middle of the arena, facing the announcer's stand.

After the grand entry and introduction, I went on over to the pavilion. Terry's wife, Monetta Jackson, helped me at the dance. We nicknamed her "Bouncerette" because she could spot a scuffle starting before the bouncers did. Everyone knew, when they saw Monetta moving fast through the crowd, that the bouncers would soon be escorting somebody out the door.

Sometimes Ken stepped in and did his own bouncing. Terri Larney's brother asked her once if Ken was a pretty tough guy. She said she didn't know, that she had never even seen Ken mad, much less in a fight.

"Why?" she asked.

Her brother said that he went to the dance, Saturday night, and started some trouble. Ken personally threw him out by the seat of his pants. He said Ken threw him so hard, he rolled down the walk way, then down the parking lot. When he finally stopped rolling, he stood up and his car was right there. So he just opened the door, got in and went home. He laughs every time he tells the story and so does Terri.[39]

The weekly dances in July, leading up to the rodeo in August, always drew large crowds. A band named Jade played on July 4. Our house band, the Country Lancers, played on July 11; followed by Mike Trimmer and the Sundown Band on July18; and Jerry Winslett and the

95

Eagle Creek Band on July 25. On August 1, Larry Gentry and his Country and Western Band played, and the rodeo opened on Wednesday, August 5.

PRCA Championship Rodeo Queen, twenty-two-year-old Kitty Dunnigan, was crowned opening night in1981. Miss Rodeo Oklahoma, Diane Griffith, made an appearance during the week. Dr. Lynn Phillips announced the rodeo events. The weather was great and everything went as planned.

We finished out the year with the weekly dances. Then on Christmas Eve, 1981, June's husband, Richard, phoned. I thought he was calling to tell us that he and June and the children on were on their way to McAlester for Christmas. I was startled to hear Richard say, "Ruth, there has been an accident but Martha June is alive."

Before I could catch my breath, I heard him saying, "Terry and Roger are dead."

I screamed and dropped the phone. Ken picked it up. Richard told him what had happened. A drunk driver crashed into June's car head-on when she was driving the children to church for the Christmas Eve pageant.

Grabbing the phone from Ken, I cried, "What about Tanya's babies? Tanya had married and now had three little girls.

"We lost all of them," Richard said, almost in a whisper. His three granddaughters were dead. Three-year-old Becky, eighteen-month-old Paula, and five-week-old Ruth Ann would never play with the dolls I sent. Tanya had named Ruth Ann after me and I never got to cuddle that precious baby in my arms.

"Who lived?" I shrieked. "Did anyone live?"

"Yes, Martha June, Tanya, and Sheilia survived," he said. He was calling from the waiting room at the University of Maryland Hospital in Baltimore where June and Tanya were airlifted by helicopter to the shock trauma unit. Richard had not seen Sheilia yet but he talked to the emergency room physician at Carroll County Hospital, Westminster, Maryland, where she had been taken by ambulance. Thankfully, Sheilia's injuries were not life-threatening and the family's assistant pastor was with her.

Richard and Ken decided that Mother and Daddy should not be alone when they were told of the deaths. We had planned to spend Christmas day with my parents and with my sister, Joan, and her husband, Olan Rodgers, from Broken Arrow. We agreed to meet Joan and Olan in the mall parking lot at McAlester. They were waiting for us when we arrived.

We cried and hugged each other and knew we must be strong for Mother and Daddy. Ken offered to be our spokesperson to my parents. Joan and I were grateful. Wiping away our tears, we got into our cars and drove over to Mother's and Daddy's to break the tragic news.

Mother was surprised that both couples drove up into the driveway at the same time. Ken said, "Dad, Mom, we better sit down. Something terrible has happened." It was the worst Christmas of our lives.

Joan and I flew to Maryland for the memorial service in January after the three survivors had been released from the hospitals. When I came back home in late January, 1982, I knew that our lives would never be the same without the boys and Tanya's babies. Somehow each of us must go on.

June began to journal. I often phoned just to hear her voice. Eventually she wrote and published the book, *The Night the Angels Cried: A Mother's True Story*. Written as a grief recovery book, using the tool of journaling, it won awards. First place by the Press Women of Texas and second place by the National Federation of Press Women.[40]

When the rodeo opened August 4, 1982, we had a good show lined up and I worked hard to see it succeed. Yet I couldn't help thinking about Tanya's little Becky the first night as I knelt down to drape the winner's sash on young Norma Bolen, the Ada Rodeo Queen. This could have been Becky's first rodeo. In fact everywhere I looked I kept seeing my nephews, Terry and Roger. Psychologists say that people who have lost a loved one find themselves searching for that missing face in the crowd. It's true.

The Winston score board was hauled in by trick rider, Roger Mawson, Fort Smith, Arkansas. For the past ten years he had performed with his horse, Cindy, wherever he was scheduled to bring the Winston score board. He started out steer roping and calf roping, but he got into clowning when his mare kept bucking him off as soon as he roped the calf. If that was what she was bent on doing, then he thought he ought to get paid for such an act.

No. 12. Winston Scoreboard stands above announcer's stand at the
Ken Lance Sports Arena.. Photo by Louise Hoehman.

The Nestea Teenage Top Hand Challenge offered $200 scholarships to the winner in each event. Many champion cowboys made their first winnings in their teens. Only forty-five rodeos were chosen. Nestea started this project in 1979 but discontinued it after 1982.

The Coors Chute-Out contributed $3500 to the Ada Pro Rodeo. The first Coors Chute-Out was held in Golden, Colorado, in 1980. In 1982 there were seventy-seven Coors Chute-Out rodeos. Shelly Burmeister was crowned Miss Coors Rodeo.

Rex Allen, Jr. was the featured entertainer on opening night, followed by Gene Watson, Thursday, Joe Stampley, Friday, and John Conlee, Saturday. Pake McEntire and the Country Cousins performed at the dance each night. Pake recorded his first album, "Rodeo Man" in 1980. We loved that album.

Pake wrote to me in 2005 sharing his memories. "The United States of America and especially folks from our great state of Oklahoma deserve a book about the legendary Ken Lance. I never heard Ken sing or play a musical instrument but when I think of Ken Lance I think entertainer. He knew how to bring us Okies out of the sticks by looking forward to coming to Ken Lance's to be entertained over and over again, each time leaving eager to come back.

"Today I can't think of anywhere to go to have a good time like we all had at Ken's. As for helping country music talents, well, Ken's just the utmost! He let Reba, Susie, and I play at the dance when we were way too young to be in there and shore too young to be special guests!

"Countless country artists contribute their success toward the help of Ken. He put us in front of Loretta Lynn when she was red hot. He got us on a CBS commercial, got us on stage at the rodeo, and the posters that went out everywhere. No entertainer gets to their top without help, and Ken has helped a bunch of us. But as far as myself and the whole McEntire bunch, thank you, Ken for the great memories. You know, it's great to have a friend and hero in the same person, and that person is Ken Lance."[41]

Ken and I divorced again after the 1982 rodeo. I packed my personal belongings into my Lincoln Town Car and drove all the way to Carlisle Barracks, Pennsylvania, where Martha June and Richard had moved in July. Carlisle Barracks was the location of the U. S .Army War College and Richard was class president.

While Richard and June attended to their multiple official duties I was able to unwind and reflect on what had happened to all of us in the past year. Their loss of their sons and granddaughters and my loss of a marriage and rodeo promotion partner. It's a wonder any of us had a dry eye. I returned to Oklahoma, and, in 1983, Ken and I decided to give our marriage one more chance. We had the divorce set aside again, as in 1976.

At the 1983 rodeo, August 3-6, Reba McEntire entertained opening night. Her favorite recording was "Up, Up to Heaven," which was her first song to reach the top

101

ten on the charts. But Reba was overjoyed when "Can't Even Get the Blues"actually rose to number one. She made three plaques with a 45 rpm recording of "Can't Even Get the Blues" centered on each one. She inscribed the plaques and sent one to Ken, one to Red Steagall, and one to Ray Bingham, who scheduled bookings for her, sometimes without even charging a fee.

Joe Stampley, who teamed with Moe Bandy in 1979 for "Just Good Ol' Boys" and "Hey, Moe, Hey, Joe" entertained August 4. Moe Bandy performed, August 5. He won the Academy of Country Music Award for Song of the Year in1980 for "It's a Cheating Situation."

The Kendalls, Royce and Jeannie, a father and daughter duo, were featured the final night, August 6. The Kendalls' second single, "Leaving on a Jet Plane," ranked in the top twenty. Their number one song in 1977, "Heaven's Just a Sin Away," received a Grammy Award and the Country Music Association's Single of the Year Award. Pake McEntire performed nightly at the rodeo and between sets at the dances.

The "clown of clowns" Quail Dobbs, Coahoma, Texas, performed his jalopy car act. Dobbs specialized in situation comedy but Jerry Don Galloway, Colleyville, Texas, concentrated on distracting the bull. Galloway remarked during an interview with Glen Hyden, *Ada Evening News,* "It's a big honor to come to Ada to work. It's one of the biggest rodeos around and all of the big names have been here."[42]

Austin Morris, owner of Morris Boot Shop, sold more children's boots at Easter and more adults' boots at rodeo time. Children outgrow their boots so fast. In the springtime the weekly jackpot ropings and small rodeos motivated families to buy new boots for their children at Easter. In August, the Morris Boot Shop saw another surge when adults wanted to get into the rodeo spirit dressing western and buying new boots to match their outfits.[43]

In 1984 Ken and I served on the Western Heritage Committee in Ada. I served from 1984 to 1986. The week's activities included live entertainment on the court house lawn, clown face painting by the rodeo clowns, and awards for the best dressed little cowgirl and cowboy. The *Ada Evening News* ran photos of these activities and the award winners.

One of the most exciting cowboy contenders at the 1984 Ada Pro Rodeo was Charles Sampson from Los Angeles, the 1982 world champion bull rider. Sampson was the first African-American to win the world title but not the first to reach the National Finals Rodeo. Myrtis Dightman reached the national finals three times and was inducted into the National Cowboy Hall of Fame in 1997. Dightman, Sampson's inspiration, was there at the finals in 1982 to congratulate him.

In 1983 Sampson nearly lost his life in a rodeo in Washington D.C. President Ronald Reagan visited him in the hospital and invited him to the White House. Sampson not only accepted the invitation upon recovery but went on to become the Sierra Circuit winner in 1984 and the Turquoise Circuit champion in 1985-86 and 1993. In 1986 he was voted the Coors Fans Favorite Cowboy. It's no wonder Timex signed him on to advertise their watches with the slogan, "Take a licking and keep on ticking." Sampson was inducted into the Pro Rodeo Hall of Fame in 1996.[44]

Prize money for the 1984 rodeo totaled $35,000 with the Winston Rodeo Series and Coors Chute-Out contributions included. The Ada Pro Rodeo was one of forty rodeos selected out of 660 rodeos sanctioned by the PRCA for the Coors Chute-Out. The rodeo contributed $7,000 and money from the entry fees. Miss Coors Rodeo, Donna Keffeler, made an appearance.

Reba McEntire was featured opening night. Bill Thompson, Mayor of Ada, declared August 1, "Reba McEntire Day." David Frizzell, brother of country celebrity, Lefty Frizzell, performed August 2. David Frizzell also debuted a hit single, "You're the Reason God Made Oklahoma," with Shelly West in 1980. They won Duo of the Year awards from the Country Music Association two consecutive years.

Pake and Susie McEntire sang August 3. Pake's latest release was, "I Can't Get Through Loving You." They had been singing at the dance since they were teenagers. Susie sent me an e-mail in 2005 of her memories of that time of her life.

She said, "My earliest recollections of going to the Ken Lance Sports Arena was when I was 12-13 years old. My father, Clark McEntire, and brother, Pake, loved to team rope, and so Ken and Ruthie would have those ropings there at the arena. Even though team roping wasn't as popular as it is today, it was still an 'all nighter.' I sat and sat through the hot day and into the cool night and then to the morning when the dew fell. They like to foundered me on team roping!

"It was a great adventure when we shot the commercial there at the arena. Lots of riding and grinning and shoots over and over. It helped prepare us in our video adventures later.

"Ken Lance Sports Arena was 'the place' to go. Maybe it was the excitement of getting to go into a bar where I was not supposed to go, but I don't think so. We got to see many famous entertainers there, got to meet really good-looking guys, and got lots of experience singing in front of a crowd. We had a built-in fan club! When we would sing, Nell Shaw and Jac McEntire would be front and center.

"Ken and Ruthie would be very hospitable–at least one set up and one big bowl of popcorn. They were always good to us kids and we appreciate them to this day."[45]

Susie released her first solo album the next year, 1985, and her husband, Paul Luchsinger was ranked the number one steer wrestler in the world the same year. Susie and Paul established the Psalms Ministry, Inc. Susie sang gospel music and she and Paul gave their Christian testimony in cowboy church services.

Moe Bandy starred August 4. This was his fourth consecutive appearance at the Ken Lance Sports Arena and his fans were there to dance to the music of the King of Honky Tonk. On the final night, Saturday, August 5, Ed Bruce and his Tennessee Cowboy Band performed.

Ed Bruce and his wife, Patsy, wrote the popular song, "Mamas Don't Let Your Babies Grow Up to Be Cowboys." Before Ed hit the big time in the entertainment industry, he worked at a used car dealership in Memphis and later moved to Nashville. There, he appeared in TV commercials and a TV movie, "The Chisholms." His next role was in the "Maverick" TV series, renamed "Bret Maverick," with James Garner.

The final night of the 1984 rodeo, four world champion steer wrestlers competed. Butch Myers, the 1980 champion, placed first. Three-time world champion, Roy Duvall, placed second. Joe Edmondson, the 1983 world champion, placed third. Dave Brock, the 1978 world champion placed fourth.

The Ada Rodeo Queen was Julie Thomas, age seventeen, from Fittstown. This was the first year the American Cancer Society held their Rodeo Queen Contest at the Ada Pro Rodeo. The contestants came from the top ten cancer fund raisers in the state. They were judged on horsemanship, personality, appearance, poise, and public speaking. They rode in the grand entry at the rodeo. The state winner was announced Saturday night.

Ken's father, Dea Lance, was still roping at eighty-four years of age. True to his promise, he had successfully taught himself to rope left handed after he lost a finger on his right hand, team roping in 1971. Since then, Dea placed in eighteen out of twenty-one local rodeos. How did he do it? He never gave up. He still had one good hand, didn't he?

Daddy suffered a similar fate in his twenties when he almost lost his left arm (Daddy was left handed) in a motorcycle accident. He begged the doctor not to take his arm. Since Daddy didn't drink or smoke, the doctor said the arm just might heal. Although his left arm became shorter than his right, Daddy strengthened both arms by playing tennis for many years.

The Shortgrass Country News voted the Ada Pro Rodeo as the top professional rodeo in the southwest. Ken and I were awarded a trophy and jackets for our management of the rodeo. It was rated one of the top five rodeos in the southwest in the past ten years and number one in three of the last five years.

The 1984 Finals of the Texoma Championship Barrel Racing were sponsored by Budweiser Light Beer at the arena, October 26-28. The producer, Ed Wild, leased the arena for the Futurity and Derby. Each year a different rodeo arena was selected for the competitive event.

By 1985 Mother and Daddy had stopped coming to the rodeo. Daddy was diagnosed with Parkinson's disease and he couldn't maneuver his way safely through the crowds with his cane. He had a couple of minor accidents in parking lots at McAlester and made the difficult decision to sell his car and retire his driver's license.

In the summer of 1985 Daddy was hospitalized with a viral illness and couldn't regain his stamina. Mother and Daddy needed help. They sold their home and most of their belongings in McAlester and rented an apartment in Broken Arrow where they could live near Joan and Olan.

June and Richard moved to Fort Monroe, Virginia, that summer where Richard became staff surgeon for the U. S. Army Training and Doctrine Command (TRADOC). Ken and I were busier than ever getting ready for the August rodeo. Joan and Olan had a full time job looking after Mother and Daddy.

The Winston score board returned for the rodeo, August 7-10, 1985. Tickets sold for $5.00 advance, $6.00 at the gate. Dance tickets sold for $5.00. Prize money totaled $43,750.

This year local entertainers got their chance to perform at the Ken Lance Sports Arena. The Red River Band from Ada was featured opening night. The Queen's Court, Debbie Allen and Judy McLelland, cousins from Ada, performed the next night. They were voted the 1984 Duet of the Year by the Oklahoma Opry, Oklahoma City. The Queen's Court appeared on several TV shows in Nashville and country music jamborees in Texas, as well as music festivals in Oklahoma.

On August 9, Steve Womack and his band sang cowboy country gospel music. They were based at Noble, Oklahoma. Saturday night, the Sour Whiskey Band from McAlester played. The Outlaw Band from the state prison played every night.

Among the big name world champion cowboy contenders were Chris Lybbert from Coyote, California; Roy Cooper from Durant, Oklahoma; Charlie Sampson from Los Angeles, California; Brad Gjermundson from Marshall, North Dakota; Bud Munore from Texas, Tom Ferguson from Miami, Oklahoma; Tea Woolman from

Fredonia, Texas; and Leo Camarillo from Lockeford, California.

Kenny Call, the 1978 world champion steer roper, competed for the fourth year. He entered the calf roping and team roping events. Born in Oklahoma City and raised in Enid, Kenny Call sponsored a steer roping school at Fittstown, home of Bill Montin. Kenny Call and Joe Miller, nephew of movie star Ben Johnson, were the instructors.

Ben Johnson once told Ken that there was money to be made in Hollywood. Ken didn't listen but Kenny did. He starred in six films in eight years and still managed to compete in rodeos when he wasn't producing a movie.

We were glad to have Don Endsley back to announce the 1985 Ada Pro Rodeo. He was the 1984 "Rodeo Master of Ceremonies" at the National Finals Rodeo in Oklahoma City. Leon and Vicki Adams returned with their specialty bull and horse act each night. Vicki's dancing horse,"One Little One," was the winner of the 1984 Specialty Act of the Year.

The Ada Rodeo Queen, Kari Henderson, Tupelo, Oklahoma, was crowned, Friday night. The American Cancer Society Rodeo Queen, Annabelle Ward, was crowned Saturday night. The American Cancer Society presented an appreciation plaque to Ken and me for hosting the American Cancer Society Special Event. All proceeds from the queen contest, raffle ticket sales, and rodeo program sales were donated to the American Cancer Society.

109

The first American Cancer Society benefit rodeo was hosted at Talihina, Oklahoma, 1980 by former Oklahoma State Representative, Don Huddleston, a cowboy and businessman. In 1982 the rodeo moved to the Seminole Roundup Club Arena. The rodeo benefit was sanctioned by the Central States Rodeo Association in 1984 and moved to the Ken Lance Sports Arena.

The final night, August 10, 1985, Ken and I shared the Honorary Attorney General title presented by Oklahoma Attorney General, Mike Turpen. Oklahoma was proud of its rodeo heritage, and elected state officials often attended the Ada Pro Rodeo.

In the fall we were fortunate to be able to book Willie Nelson for a concert in the arena, October 5. Tickets sold for $15.00. He was such a huge success nationwide in the 1980s, playing for charitable causes. He performed in the videotape, "We Are the World," recorded for the "USA for Africa" fund raiser for famine relief in Africa.

Willie was scheduled to come to us right after the Farm Aid concert he organized in Champaign, Illinois. But he was totally exhausted and came down with pneumonia, and had to cancel his date with us for October 5. When Willie cancelled, our helpers at the dance pavilion cancelled too. Yet we knew we could still expect the usual Saturday night dance crowd. Our house band, Silver Wings, didn't desert us. Ken phoned Monetta and Terry Jackson, who had moved to Tyler, Texas, and told them our situation. They got in touch with Karen and Bob Coleman and the four of them showed up to help us at the dance.

Willie rescheduled the concert for, November 3, and made his eighth appearance at the Ken Lance Sports Arena. Tickets for the canceled concert were honored.

No. 13. Willie Nelson in concert at the Ken Lance Sports Arena. Photo by Louise Hoehman.

Willie knew that Ken would have a hard time paying him in full because of the rescheduling. Therefore he didn't demand his fee in advance. Willie told Ken to pay him when he could and left without sticking around to find out how much Ken might have been able to pay that night.

Ken saved his money after every dance and the next rodeo until the bills filled a gunny sack. Two years later Willie was scheduled to do a concert at Oral Roberts University in Tulsa. Ken drove to Tulsa in a heavy rainstorm and found Willie's band trailer. He banged on the door and hollered, "It's Ken Lance out here, guys." Paul English, the drummer, opened the door and shouted, "Ken Lance, get in here out of the rain."

Willie was stranded somewhere else until the storm cleared, so Ken handed the gunny sack to Paul. Paul laughed when he gripped the dripping sack but I don't think he was surprised. Ken brought personalized belt buckles for each member of the band. I don't think anyone ever let him forget that night, especially the band member whose name didn't show up on a belt buckle. But Ken made good on it at a later time.

On Sunday, June 1, 1986, the George Strait and Tanya Tucker Concert was held in the arena, presented by the Little Win and Proctor Promotions, Texas. Tickets sold for $13.50 advance, and $15.00 at the gate. In spite of the light rain during the entire concert, the arena was packed so tight that hundreds of people sat on camp chairs on the arena's dirt floor. Several times police had to ask them to move back from the stage.

Tanya Tucker sang the first hour. Among the songs she sang were, "San Antonio Stroll," "Delta Dawn," "Ridin' Rainbows," "It's a Cowboy Lovin' Night," and her latest hit, "One Love at a Time."

George Strait performed the second hour. He sang "You Look So Good in Love," "Let's Fall to Pieces Together," "Does Fort Worth Ever Cross Your Mind?" and "Nobody in His Right Mind Would Have Left Her."

In August, the Ada Pro Rodeo featured Becky Hobbs opening night with her band, Oklahoma Heart. In 1985 she was nominated for the top new female vocalist award by the Academy of Country Music. She made more than 25 TV appearances.

Pake and Susie McEntire entertained, Thursday. They released a cassette together in 1983. Pake's first single, "Every Night," was a top twenty hit. He had three top twenty hits. He released two RCA albums in 1985, "Too Old to Grow Up Now," and "My Whole World." Pake's latest hit was "Saving My Love for You."

Con Hunley performed, Friday. The Academy of Country Music nominated him for most promising male vocalist. His greatest success was, "Oh, Girl." Con Hunley opened concerts for Tammy Wynette, George Jones, the Oak Ridge Boys, and Alabama and the Judds.

Saturday, August 9, 1986, Rebecca Holden was the parade marshall and Mayor Clint Sturdevant proclaimed, "Rebecca Holden Day"in Ada. Don Endsley, rodeo announcer, was the master of ceremonies for the parade.

Rebecca Holden was featured at the rodeo and dance that night. The Sour Whiskey band played every night.

The stock contractor was the Bad Rodeo Stock Company owned by Mack Altizer from Sonora, Texas, and Rudy Vela from Edinburg, Texas. They brought bulls and horses that had been ridden in the National Finals Rodeo.

Among the bulls they brought were Saturday Night Live, Big Bend Coors, Bad to the Bone, and Savage Seven. Their bucking horses were Mile High, Rojo, Happy Trails, and Hellsapoppin.' Since the bucking horse or bull as well as the rider is judged, contenders want to draw a real challenger.

The American Federal Savings & Loan Company in Ada sponsored the drawing for the wheelbarrow-full-of-money giveaway. Miss Rodeo Oklahoma, Teresa Carle from Noble, Oklahoma, appeared Wednesday and Thursday nights. Patty Wallenberg from Moore, Oklahoma, appeared each night with her trained horse, "Painted Magic."

U. S. Representatives Jim Jones and Wes Watkins, State Senator Billie Floyd, and State Representative Lonnie Abbot were present at the rodeo. I should have known something was up but I was so busy dashing over to the pavilion to be sure everything was in order for the dance, that I didn't mention it to Ken.

As it turned out Ken and I were honored with a citation for our work in promoting rodeo in Oklahoma, but I wasn't there. U. S. Representatives Jim Jones and Wes Watkins presented the American flag to Ken that had flown over the nation's capitol in Washington, D.C. Oklahoma Senator Billie Floyd and Oklahoma Representative Lonnie Abbot presented the flag to Ken that flew over the state capitol in Oklahoma City.

After the 1986 rodeo, I felt like I was suffering from post traumatic stress. My frequent trips to Broken Arrow were depressing as I realized that Daddy's condition could only worsen. Mother was alone for the first time in her life. The rodeo had lost its attraction for me after the deaths of my nephews and Tanya's children. My whole world was spinning out of control.

I left Ken on August 28 and moved to Durant, Oklahoma. Ken hired two men to move my furniture in a U-Haul truck. Ken drove to Durant in my car with me. It was sad when the guys unloaded my furniture and we knew that this was it. We both were in tears. We made a promise to each other that, although our marriage was over, we would always be there for each other as friends.

On September 8, 1986, our divorce was granted. This time it was final. I drove to Paris, Texas, where Richard and June had bought a ranch for their eventual retirement. With me I brought gifts for the family. These were the souvenir covered wagon TV lamps. The words, "Ken Lance Sports Arena, Ada, Oklahoma," were painted in red on each side of the canvas covering. Since Ken was a calf roper, team roper, and trick roper, the cowboy painted on the covered wagon could have been Ken getting off his horse to rope.

June hugged me at the ranch and said, "Ruth, your world is crumbling, yet you come bearing gifts for us." June said that the covered wagon was the most meaningful thing I could have given them, especially to her son, Mike, who remembered riding in Ken's covered wagon back in 1964, advertising the first Ada rodeo in the new Ken Lance Sports Arena.

Richard and June took me with them back to Fort Monroe, Virginia, for a long visit. During that time, I came to terms with my grief and the divorce, and began to plan for a new life. When I returned to Oklahoma, I made my home in Durant and for the next five years I worked at the Quality Inn Motel as the Director of Sales.

The George Strait and Tanya Tucker concert in the arena was so successful in 1986 that Ken booked another George Strait arena concert, June 7, 1987. Kathy Mattea sang the first hour. The Country Music Association named George Strait the Male Vocalist of the Year in 1985 and 1986 and again in1989 and1990. Among his number one hits were "Amarillo by Morning," "A Fire I Can't Put Out," "You Look So Good in Love," "Right or Wrong," and "It Ain't Cool to be Crazy About You."

Promotion was all I had ever known in the rodeo business and so I agreed to promote the 1987 Ada Pro Rodeo in Durant on the radio and in the news media. Ken appreciated the promotions I secured in Bryan County.

At the rodeo, August 5-8, a number of PRCA champion cowboys entered the competition: Monty "Hawkeye" Henson, three-time world champion saddle bronc rider; Don Gay, eight-time world champion bull rider; Tuff Hedeman, the current world champion bull rider; Roy Cooper, eight-time world champion calf roper; and Lane Frost, who won the 1987 world champion bull rider title in the National Finals Rodeo in December.

The stock contractor, Mack Althizer's Bad Company Rodeo from Sonora, Texas, returned. He brought his stock directly from the Cheyenne Frontier Days. The McAlester prison band performed nightly to promote the September prison rodeo. The Coca Cola Classic awarded $100 to the winner in each event and belt buckles to kids in the calf scramble. The drawing for the wheelbarrow full of money each night was a popular attraction and a lot of fun for the winner.

We always had an ambulance present at the rodeo but no cowboy wanted to be taken to the emergency room. He wanted to get back on his horse and win some prize money. Therefore, the Justin Boot Company, Fort Worth, Texas, sponsored the Justin Heeler/PRCA Pro Rodeo Sports Medicine Program and designed a mobile medical unit equipped to stabilize the injured cowboy and turn him loose. The Ada Pro Rodeo was one of about twenty rodeos selected by the program.

The Justin Heeler program started in 1981 and the mobile medical center was introduced at the 1982 National Finals Rodeo. The Justin Boot Company was the exclusive manufacturer of the official boot and belt line of the PRCA.

Improvements were made at the dance pavilion also. Two dressing rooms were added to the west side of the stage so the stars could change clothes quickly. Mel McDaniel, a native Oklahoman, was the featured entertainer opening night with two hugely successful albums out, "Let It Roll" and "Stand Up." His number one hit single was, "Baby's Got Her Blue Jeans On."

Thursday night, the seven-piece band, Asleep at the Wheel, reminiscent of Bob Wills, played. Their latest hit single was, "House of Blue Lights," from their album, "Asleep at the Wheel 10." They played everything from honky-tonk to boogie, blues, and country rock.

Friday night, Dan Seals played country and pop and his hit singles from his late 1985 album, "Won't Be Blue Anymore," "Meet Me in Montana," "Everything That Glitters (Is Not Gold)" and "Bop." In 1976 he sang as England Dan, with John Ford Coley, "I'd Really Love to See You Tonight," which sold two million copies.

Saturday, the parade marshals were the Riders in the Sky, the featured entertainers at the rodeo and dance. This trio was made up of yodeler, Doug Green; fiddler, Paul Chrstman; and ball player and comedy "varmint" dancer, Fred "Too Slim" LaBour. "Too Slim" danced imitating the armadillo, jack rabbit, and the draped sloth. Randy Weeks and his band, Destiny, played each night.

Trick roper, Joyce Rice from North Hollywood, California, was the specialty act. The bull fighter clown was Tony Johnson and the barrel man was Michael "Smurf" Horton from Zolfo Springs, Florida.

The year closed with the Ada Christmas parade, December 1,1987. Ken was invited to serve as parade marshal. They called him, "The Electric Cowboy," when he rode his fiber glass horse decorated with Christmas Lights. He won second place.

In 1988,the Ada Pro Rodeo, August 3-6, was supported in part by Coors, the Coca Cola Classic, and Wrangler Pro Rodeo. The nightly calf scramble was open to kids eight to twelve years old.

Ricky Van Shelton was featured opening night. With thirteen consecutive hit singles and four albums selling more than one million copies each, he received the Horizon award as country's most promising newcomer. The next year, the Country Music Association selected him Male Vocalist of the Year. Among his hit songs were "Crime of Passion," "Somebody Lied," "Life Turned Her That Way," and "She's Not Your Baby Anymore."

Gene Watson performed, August 4. Moe Bandy played Friday night. The International Rodeo Association (IRA) selected Moe Bandy the Entertainer of the Year. The Rodeo Cowboys Association (RCA) named him Texas Entertainer of the Year. Fans remembered him for his 1974 hit, "I Just Started Hatin' Cheatin' Songs Today," which launched his career as a country music singer.

In 1980 Moe Bandy and Joe Stampley won the Vocal Duo of the Year award from the Country Music Association and in 1980 and 1981 from the Academy of Country Music. Moe Bandy competed in bull riding and bareback bronc riding in rodeos for several years but it was his brother, Mike, who made it to the PRCA National Finals Rodeo seven years in the bull riding event. Moe

Bandy's rodeo songs included "Rodeo Romeo" and "Someday Soon."

Saturday morning, Red Steagall was the parade marshal for the Ada Western Heritage Parade. Saturday night, Red and his band, the Coleman County Cowboys, entertained at the rodeo and the dance.

No. 14. Red Steagall , Official Cowboy Poet of Texas, singer, songwriter, and popular radio host of Cowboy Corner. Photo by Louise Hoehman.

Over 200 of the songs Red Steagall composed were also recorded by other singers. His voice was the principal speaking role in the Disney film, "Benjie, the Hunter." In addition to each night's featured entertainer, the Stonehorse Band played at the dances.

The rodeo announcer, Charlie Throckmorton from Grandview, Texas, was a steer roper before he turned to rodeo announcing. With his background as a life member of the Pro Rodeo Historical Society, Charlie had an endless supply of interesting stories and statistics to tell when he wasn't rapidly explaining what was happening in the arena.

World famous trick roper, J. W. Stoker, made his entrance on his white horse, jumping through a large paper horseshoe, with Stoker spinning seventy-five feet of rope around himself and the horse. This trick was called the Cowboy Wedding Ring. Stoker's horse, Hot Diggity, did some rope spinning of his own by holding the rope in his mouth while he was spinning it.

For more than thirty years, Stoker traveled worldwide, performing his trick roping in Cuba, the Dominican Republic, Venezuela, Europe, and Japan. In the United States he performed in Madison Square Garden and in the big livestock shows in Denver, Fort Worth, and Houston.

Stoker appeared in a couple of movies; on the David Frost Show; and in ABC's special coverage of the Olympics. In 1976 he performed on the Mike Douglas Show while Larry Mahan sang. In 1988 Stoker performed at the Calgary Olympics Rodeo.

121

Miss Rodeo Oklahoma, Susie Gippert made an appearance at the 1988 rodeo. Candis Clark sang the National Anthem, Friday and Saturday. The stock contractor was Bernis Johnson, Johnson Rodeo Company. He brought his horse, the Skoal's Sippin' Velvet, six times Bareback Horse of the Year, for the cowboys to ride in the Pro Ada Rodeo.

Brenda Revels and her sister, Karen Thornberry, competed in the team roping event. It was the first time that women had entered this event at the Ada Pro Rodeo.

Among the champions competing that year were Tuff Hedeman, 1986 world champion bull rider; Martha Josey, three-time world champion barrel racer; Bud Monroe, 1987 Dodge Circuit saddle bronc champion; Dave Appleton, 1986 world champion saddle bronc rider; Richard Stowers, former world champion calf roper; and Lane Frost, the 1987 world champion bull rider.

Lane Frost was the first and only man to ride Red Rock, the 1988 PRCA Bucking Bull of the Year, in a series of seven promotional rodeos, "The Challenge of the Champions." Red Rock belonged to John Growney and Don Kish. In 312 previous attempts, no other rider had been able to stay on that bull for eight seconds.

Tragically, on July 30, 1989, at the Cheyenne Frontier Days, the bull, "Takin' Care of Business," took care of Lane Frost. He gored him in the back, broke his ribs, and pierced a vital artery. The bull came from the livestock provided by Bad Company Rodeo. Frost never heard what he had scored.

Ken attended Lane's funeral at Hugo, Oklahoma. He couldn't believe that this twenty-four-year-old cowboy champion was dead. Only last year Lane had entered the bull riding event at the Ken Lance Sports Arena. Lane was buried next to his hero and mentor, Freckles Brown.

Ironically, Freckles died March 30, 1987, the same year that Frost won his world bull rider title. Lane considered his dad and Freckles Brown and Don Gay to be his best teachers. The movie, *Eight Seconds*, documented Lane's brief rodeo career.

The 1980s closed without the annual Ada rodeo in 1989. Ken's health was bad. He thought his rodeo days were over. Ken and Lola June, a former wife, remarried. She was a widow and lived nearby. *The Ada Times* ran an editorial,"Hey, Ken, It's Rodeo Time."

> We don't know about you, but things didn't seem quite the same this week without Ken Lance and his world famous, Ada PRCA rodeo. . . . Perhaps our readers missed going to the rodeo, seeing the big downtown parade and the stars just like us. Ken Lance was the spark that made it happen. He rebuilt the rodeo system from the ground up in our area. We missed you, Ken, this year and hope that things will get back on track for 1990.[47]

On December 10, 1989, Daddy died. Mother and Daddy had moved back to McAlester in 1987 where she rented an apartment across the street from the nursing home. Daddy's health improved until he was hospitalized with pneumonia in December, 1989. Joan drove down to McAlester from Broken Arrow and I drove up from Durant where I was working as Director of Sales at the Quality Inn.

June and Richard were living in El Paso, Texas. Richard had been promoted to the rank of brigadier general in 1988 and was the Commanding General of William Beaumont Army Medical Center. June consulted with the doctor by phone and planned to fly out before Christmas. The doctor said that Daddy was cheerful that morning and he thought he would probably survive the pneumonia. June made her reservations on American Airlines. Joan and I went home with Mother to get some sleep after kissing Daddy good night.

The phone on Mother's bedside table rang about 5:00 a.m. She answered it and screamed. "He's gone. Lowell's gone." Mother didn't wait for Joan or me to call anyone. She called June. A few hours later June was flying on the first available airlines to Tulsa where Joan's husband, Olan Rodgers, met her plane and drove her down to McAlester. It was December 10, 1989. Richard arrived the day of the funeral.

Although Ken had remarried, it somehow seemed right for him to join my family in our grief. We had repaid our loan to Daddy before we divorced in 1986 but the repayment and our divorce did not mark the end of their relationship. Ken had even visited Daddy in the nursing home. My nieces and nephews still called him, "Uncle Ken." He came and was welcomed to sit with the family.

124

It was bitterly cold and overcast the day of the funeral. Icicles hung from the trees. At the close of the Masonic funeral service, when the mourners walked past the casket, Richard stopped and removed his silver star from his brigadier general's uniform. He dropped the star into Daddy's suit pocket over his heart. Daddy always believed in Richard and his medical military career just as he always believed in Ken and me in our rodeo production career.

The show would go on in the 1990s but in a very different way for each of us. The sun shone briefly at the cemetery. An omen?

CHAPTER IV.

Reining in the Dream in the 1990s

Although Ken didn't produce a rodeo in 1989, neither he nor Ada was ready for him to retire. Therefore, Ken put together a three-day rodeo. He served on the 1990 Ada Western Heritage Committee, and helped to organize a whole week of western-style activities involving the local businesses, ending with a parade on the final date of the rodeo.

What better way to launch the celebration of Western Heritage Week than with a good old fashioned country music jubilee at the Music Palace featuring local talent? On Western Heritage Sunday, the public was invited to hear Susie (McEntire) Luchsinger and her husband Paul, a champion PRCA steer roper, give their testimony and concert at Evangelistic Temple.

Local businesses offered discounts on almost anything western. Free rodeo tickets were offered with certain purchases. Employees dressed in western style all week and awards were given for the best dressed employee and the best decorated store window.

Ken threw his heart into bringing back the Ada Rodeo to cheering crowds at the Ken Lance Sports Arena, the week of August 2-4. He teamed with entertainer and roper, Shane Barmby, as his roping partner. Ken's dad, Dea Lance, was ninety years old and had roped his last team roping event with Ken in 1988.

Shane grew up singing and roping in a musically talented rodeo family. While Ken was starting to rein in his dream in rodeo production in Oklahoma, Shane was roping and riding his dream to country music stardom out of Nashville.

Movie star, Becky Hobbs, gave Shane his big break when she invited him to play a cowboy role in her video, "Are There Any More Like You (Where You Come From")? What's more, her video producer, Mary Matthews, agreed to manage Shane's singing career.

Shane Barmby was the parade marshal in downtown Ada, Saturday, August 4, and the featured entertainer at the rodeo and dance that night. He was best known for the song, "A Rainbow of Our Own," from his first album, "Let's Talk About Us." The album was produced by Bud Logan on PolyGram.

After the dance, Ken paid Terri Larney one hundred dollars to drive Shane to the Dallas-Fort Worth airport. Terri was thrilled. She drove home singing, "Happy Birthday to Me," since it really was her birthday and driving Barmby was like a birthday wish come true.

Terri's best friend, Belinda Parshall, worked in the office as Ken's administrative assistant from 1986 to 1993. Her husband, Richard, worked the concession stand from 1990 to 1993. Ken had a policy of accepting no checks for entry fees. Too many cowboys wrote bad checks, counting on winning the cash to make good their checks.

In the old days Ken would pay the fees himself for some of the local cowboys, but Ken couldn't do that anymore. One young cowboy was insulted when Belinda refused his personal check.

"Do you know who I am?" he demanded.

"No, I don't," she replied in her best business-like voice, "but there are no exceptions to the No Check policy."

Suddenly, Ken stepped forward, red-faced, and smiled sheepishly at the cowboy. Speaking in a squeaky voice, he said, "Belinda, I'll stand good for this cowboy's check. This is Ty Murray, the 1989 all-around champion cowboy of the world." Ty's rodeo earnings in 1989 alone totaled $134,806.

Belinda was impressed with his title and his bank account but not with his claiming exception to the rules. Neither was the Professional Bull Riders organization a few years later in 1999. Although Ty was a founding member of the PBR, he had to forfeit his entry in the short go for the finals in the Houston Livestock Show & Rodeo when it conflicted with a PBR event on the same date.

According to PBR rules members could not be excused from a PBS event except for medical reasons under a doctor's orders; medical reasons for a family member; or a death in the family. A conflict in event dates could not be excused.[48]

The entertainers in 1990 were young, appealing to the younger generation of rodeo fans. The bouncers at the dances were younger too. Ken's niece, Sandi Lance, who baby-sat Loretta Lynn's twin daughters in the early days of the rodeo, married Ray Sanders. Sandi and Ray had a son, Shannon Ray Sanders, who worked as a bouncer at the dance pavilion.

Six feet, four inches tall, Shannon could see over the heads of most of the crowd. He found that the girls fought dirtier than the guys. He would separate them by grabbing each one under the arm and lifting her off the floor. The girls couldn't fight if they couldn't reach each other. But that didn't keep one angry female from landing her fist on Shannon's nose and cracking it.

Gospel singer, John Arnold, and the John Arnold Band were featured on opening night, Thursday, August 2. They were the winners of the National Wrangler Country Showdown competition in Nashville in 1983. The group released their first single, "How We Gonna Know It's Love?" in 1984 on the Compleat record label distributed by PolyGram. John Arnold was named the 1989 Male Vocalist of the Year by the Oklahoma Opry Association. Randy Weeks and the Sour Whiskey Band played every night during the rodeo.

Larry Boone was featured Friday, August 3. Among his most popular recordings were "Everybody Wants to be Hank Williams," "Don't Give Candy to a Stranger," and "Paradise." Boone opened shows for Merle Haggard and George Jones. He lettered in football, basketball, and baseball in high school. He graduated from Florida Atlanta University with a degree in physical education. He was nominated Favorite New Country Artist by the fans at the American Music Awards.

In 1990 I returned to the Ada rodeo on the final night at the request of friends. They said there had been a good turnout both nights at the rodeo. I was glad to see that the Coca Cola Classic was still awarding $100 to the winner in each event and belt buckles to the winners in the calf scramble for children ages eight to twelve. Local businesses were still sponsoring the wheelbarrow full of money since the mid-1980s.

Much had changed, also, since I left in 1986. Gone was the Winston electronic scoreboard. The kids I knew in the sixties and seventies, who played with my nieces and nephews, had kids of their own now. In fact many couples met their future spouses at the dances.

We shared memories. We all remembered the clown barrel man, Tommy Lucia from Weatherford, Texas. He performed a contract act in the arena in 1976 with his swayback horse, "Old Paint." Now it was his son, Tommy Joe, who performed with his dad's famous swayback horse. The elder Lucia appeared in the movies, "Junior Bonner" and "The Great American Cowboy."

Bull fighter Jimmy Anderson performed his act with his working sheepdog and cowboy monkey. The monkey wore a tiny cowboy hat, western shirt, and chaps and rode on the back of the sheepdog. Like they say, "Monkey see, monkey do."

Jimmy Anderson was one of the PRCA's top bull fighters with eleven years experience performing on the Wrangler Pro Rodeo Bullfighters Tour. He was named the

National Rodeo Finals Bullfighter two times and the Canadian National Finals Rodeo Bullfighter three times.

I didn't know rodeo announcer, John Shipley, from Steamboat Springs, Colorado. The PRCA announcers must qualify for an apprentice status leading to certification as a PRCA announcer. John Shipley was certified in 1988 and ran the press room one year at the National Finals Rodeo. He was a bareback rider who loved to ride but he found his talent in rodeo announcing.

Stock contractors, Chris and Janie Hedlund, owners of the Hedlund Rodeo Company, Montezuma, Kansas, rode in the grand entry as the Hedlund Wranglers, with their daughters, Brit, Amy, and Heidi, and their son, Payson. I always liked to see a family working and riding together. The Hedlund livestock was top quality. Two of their bulls had bucked off champion cowboys in the National Finals Rodeo in Las Vegas.

The cover of the rodeo program advertised the Justin Heeler Sports Medicine Program and Justin boots. It was always reassuring to the cowboys and cowgirls to see the Justin Heeler mobile unit. No more time out for a trip to the emergency room. Fortunately, no one was ever killed by a bull in the Ken Lance Sports Arena but there were occasional injuries.

The week following the rodeo, the *Ada Evening News* ran an editorial congratulating the entire community on the success of Western Heritage Week.

"With Ken Lance getting back into full stride with his annual star spangled rodeo and the many promotions held in downtown Ada that everyone enjoyed, it was the best in years.

"Many people don't realize just how much an event such as the rodeo means to our area. The motels were doing well and the cash registers throughout the business community were singing. Tourism is big business and events such as this one can do nothing but help our sluggish economy. Congratulations on a job well done!"[49]

Meanwhile, on April 4, 1991, I married Dr. John T. Krattiger. He was the retired Dean of Men and Vice President of Student Services, Southeastern Oklahoma State University, Durant. John taught mathematics and coached tennis at the university for many years. He retired in 1984.

Both John and I were Red Coat Ambassadors for the Durant Chamber of Commerce. We enjoyed an active life in Kiwanis, university-related social events, and Episcopal church activities. I retired in 1992 from the position of Director of Sales at Quality Inn, Durant

Although I did not attend the Ada rodeo in 1991, I kept up with the news through friends and newspaper articles. Becky Hobbs returned to play opening night, August 7. Doug Stone was featured, August 8; Marty Stuart, August 9; and Dean Dillon, August 10. The Stonehorse Band of Tulsa played every night at the dance. The Stonehorse Band was chosen the Entertainer of the Year by the International Professional Rodeo Association.

Dean Dillon shared parade marshal honors with Montie Montana, world-famous trick roper and movie star.

A young trick roper, Kyle Lane, was convinced that Ken rewarded his young protégé by contracting Montie to perform at the annual Ada rodeo. Like Ken, Montie gave Kyle some valuable tips on trick roping.

Montie rode Ken's horse but Ken did not have time to polish the silver conches on the saddle. Montie bought a can of silver polish and shined the silver himself. He gave the can to Ken with a message he wrote on the top of the cardboard box, "To Ken, the P.T. Barnum of Rodeo."

Maybe that's why Ken later allowed a circus to rent the arena for a show. He would never do that again. Two days before the circus, six elephants were staked outside the entrance to the arena to attract ticket buyers. After the matinee and evening performances the circus owner requested permission to leave his elephants staked in the pasture a few days. The elephants stunk up the entire neighborhood for two months after they left. Whew! The dance customers didn't appreciating the lingering odor.

Kyle said that Ken loved everything about rodeoing and he was always teaching someone. "We practiced trick roping on the hardwood floor in the dance hall. Ken told me that rope would take me as far as I was willing to go. When he thought I was good enough, he introduced me to Ray Bingham. Ray got me some contracts and I owe it all to Ken. That's the kind of friend Ken was."[50]

Ken's dad, Dea Lance, taught Kyle to team rope when Kyle was a teenager. Dea and Kyle team roped together at several rodeos. After 1988, when Dea was no longer able to compete, Kyle team roped with Ken.

Jim McLain from Duncan, Oklahoma, was the bull fighter clown for the 1991 rodeo. He wrote his own material for his contract act in which he played the roles of three characters: Will Turdley, Cow Patty, and Gabor Dundee. McAlin started his bullfighter career in 1980 and two years later the *Shortgrass Country News* voted him the Rodeo Clown of the Year.

In 1987 McLain was the bull fighter chosen for the Prairie Circuit Rodeo Finals in Guthrie, Oklahoma, and for the National Old Timers Rodeo Finals in Amarillo, Texas. He placed among the top three in eighty-seven percent of all open bullfighting contests he entered from 1985 to 1990. McLain was sponsored by Miller Lite.

Coca Cola sponsored the girls' barrel racing event, sanctioned by the WPRA (Women's Professional Rodeo Association). The competition was part of the Wrangler Circuit Series and the purse was $1,100. All the contenders rode in the grand entry. Stock producers, Chris and Janie Hedlund from Montezuma, Kansas, again provided the livestock. Don Ensley introduced the rodeo guests and announced the events in his lively style.

Ken's dad regretted that he was unable to see the rodeo due to his poor health. On November 6, 1991, Dea Lance died at the age of ninety-one. Tony Pippen, columnist for the *Ada Evening News*, wrote in his column that "Lance died without fanfare, but he had his fans–including me. I not only admired his stamina, but his love for what he did. It undoubtedly kept him younger than his age indicated."[51]

Only Ken was left of the original foursome–our dads, Ken and me–to keep the rodeo going. The time was near for Ken to rein in the dream he had roped for three decades. His hair had turned white, yet his spirit was as young and hopeful as it had always been.

Somehow Ken was energized by the smell of leather and horses, the rumble of livestock trailers, and the sight of old friends returning faithfully to carry on the multitude of behind-the-scene tasks that produced a great rodeo every year.

Ken knew that a cowboy on the ground keeps getting up as long as he can pull himself together. Therefore, he looked ahead, as he had always done, to a bigger and better rodeo next year. The rodeo poster was different in 1992. Ken's picture was centered on a wagon wheel with the spokes pointing to the pictures of the entertainers for each night. A border at the bottom of the poster displayed the photos of the stock producer, rodeo announcer, bands, and the National Anthem singers.

As always, Ken served on the Western Heritage Week committee. In all the flurry of reports and motions passed in the meetings, one piece of business was left unfinished. No one was named to receive the Ada Western Heritage Week Award of Merit. This disturbed Ken.

The award was always announced and presented at the Country Music Jubilee at Ada's Music Palace the week before the rodeo. Ken sat with one of his roping buddies that night, Oklahoma County District Attorney, Bob Macy. Ken was surprised when Bob was asked to approach the microphone. He was even more surprised when Bob

135

summoned him and announced that the committee had selected Ken Lance to receive the Ada Western Heritage Week Award of Merit. How did they do that without his suspecting something? Who says that a committee can't keep a secret?

Ken dedicated his award to the memory of his dad, Dea Lance, who died nine months earlier. Bob Macy also read a proclamation from Ada Mayor Paul Alford proclaiming Ken Lance Day in Ada, and letters of congratulations from Montie Montana and other celebrities. Pake McEntire came to the microphone and read a letter from Reba congratulating Ken. The committee had done a fine job of notifying everyone and swearing everyone to secrecy.

Our faithful friend, Nell Shaw, invited me to visit her at the 1992 rodeo. I was glad to see that Belinda Parshall and her husband, Richard, were still doing a great job, as always, with the office duties and concession sales. Ken depended on them a lot. Familiar publicity photos of the stars of long ago still decorated the office walls, along with pictures of the current entertainers.

Ken had made a new friend in Pat Turner. In the mid-1980s Pat was hired by the state prison warden to get together a rodeo committee at McAlester to promote the annual prison rodeo on Labor Day weekend. "I want Ken Lance on that committee," the warden told him.

"I don't know Ken Lance," said Pat, a newcomer to McAlester.

"Then get to know him," the warden ordered.

Pat did and he never regretted it. Pat became Ken's shadow. In the last years of Ken's life, Pat appointed himself Ken's personal chauffeur and valet to drive him and his hat boxes, boot bags, and hang-up outfits anywhere Ken wanted to go. Ken was known for his fancy wardrobe.

Pam Queen, staff member of *Pro Rodeo World*, remembered, "Ken was always decked out in his Porter Wagner attire. He rode horseback in the grand entry looking like Roy Rogers or Gene Autry." Even Reba commented on his satin shirts and sweet-smelling cologne.[52]

Since taking care of the dance pavilion was always my responsibility during the twenty-two years Ken and I operated the Ken Lance Sports Arena together, I was always interested to know what celebrities were performing. In 1992 Ken decided to feature local musicians, like he had done back in the seventies with the Singing McEntires. Now it was the next generation of Singing McEntires–Pake and his daughters, Autumn, Calamity, and Chism–who sang the National Anthem at the rodeo.

Opening night was billed as Family Night in the arena with a special concert featuring the Sweethearts of the Rodeo, sisters, Janis Gill and Kristine Arnold. Five songs from their 1986 debut album, "Sweethearts of the Rodeo," were hits that resulted in TV appearances. Fans especially liked "Chains of Gold," "Midnight Girl/Sunset Town," and "Since I Found You." On their latest album,

"Buffalo Zone," they recorded several of their top ten hits, "I Feel Fine," "Satisfy You," and "Blue to the Bone."

Fiddler, Clinton Gregory, entertained, August 6, with songs from his hit record and video, "Play, Ruby, Play." When you heard his fiddling, it was, "dance, feet, dance."You just had to kick up your heels. Much of the rodeo audience shared his sentiments in his song, "If It Weren't for Country Music I'd Go Crazy." Although Clinton Gregory was born in Martinsville, Virginia, he moved to Nashville like all country western singers do sooner or later. He signed with Step One Records for his first recording, "Music 'N' Me."

Martin Delray from Texarkana, Arkansas, was featured Friday, August 7. He played country music in high school and rock 'n roll in college where he earned a bachelor's degree in political science at the University of Arkansas. After a tour of duty in the U. S. Marine Corps, he released his debut album, "Get Rhythm," with Johnny Cash singing with him, Cash's classic, "Get Rhythm.

Saturday, August 8, the McCarter Sisters–Jennifer and her twin sisters, Lisa and Teresa–entertained. They rode in the parade in Ada as parade marshals. Clinton Gregory played with their road band in 1987 when they moved from their hometown of Sevierville, Tennessee, to Nashville. Dolly Parton was also from Sevierville and welcomed them as guest stars on "The Dolly Parton Show" in California. The McCarter sisters toured Europe with Randy Travis when their first single, "Timeless and True Love," climbed to number five on the charts. The harmony of these three sisters was fantastic.

The award-winning bull fighter clowns were Gary "Roach" Hedeman from Bowie, Texas; James Pierce from Thibideaux, Louisiana; and Kevin Davis from Battiest, Oklahoma. Hedeman was chosen by the top fifteen bull riders in Texas to fight bulls at the1989 Texas Circuit Finals in Fort Worth. He was also selected for the Wrangler Bullfight at Cheyenne Frontier Days in 1988 and 1989. At the Ada Pro Rodeo Hedeman performed a specialty act with Trigger, his palomino pony, and Buster the Beach Dog, his red heeler.

James Pierce was voted the 1985 Tri-State Rodeo Association Bullfighter of the Year. He was selected to fight bulls in the finals in Louisiana, Mississippi, and Alabama the following three years.

PRCA rodeo announcer, Don Endsley, introduced an exciting list of world champions who competed in the seven events. Oklahoma's "Million Dollar Cowboy," Roy Cooper from Durant, earned a recording breaking total of $1,282,874 during his rodeo career from 1976 to 1991. In 1983 Cooper was the world champion all-around cowboy. He also held world titles in calf roping.

Other world champion who competed at the Ada Pro Rodeo were the 1990-1991 saddle bronc rider, Robert Etbauer from Goodwell, Oklahoma; the1990 world champion bareback rider, Chuck Logue from Decatur, Texas; and the National Finals Rodeo finalist in bareback riding, Shawn Fry from Norman, Oklahoma.

Top riders in the saddle bronc event included former world champion, Tom Reeves from Stephenville, Texas; Derek Clark from Colcord, Oklahoma, sixth in the nation at that time; and Robert Etbauer and Billy Etbauer. Billy was in the lead for a world championship.

Among the top contenders in bull riding were Cody Custer from Wicksburg, Arizona; Scott Mendes from Athens, Texas; David Fournier from Decatur, Texas; and David Bailey from Tahlequah, Oklahoma.

Competing in the calf roping events were world champion calf roper Fred Whitfield from Cypress, Texas; past world champion Joe Beaver from Huntsville, Texas (1985, 1987-1988); Mike and Gary Johnson from Henryetta, Oklahoma, who reached the national finals several times; and Morris Ledford from Comanche, Oklahoma, who was ranked twelfth at that time.

World champion steer wrestler, Ote Berry (1985, 1990-1991) from Checotah, Oklahoma; three-time world champion team roper, Tee Woolman from Llano, Texas; Charles Pogue from Ringling, Oklahoma; and Steve Northcutt from Odessa, Texas, also competed.

In the barrel racing event Tracy Hedeman from Bowie, Texas, and Martee Pruitt from Minatare, Nebraska, were listed in the top twenty in the nation. Beth Braudrick from Terrell, Texas, also was a promising contender.

This was the first year that the Andrews Rodeo Company provided the stock. B. D. Andrews was a top PRCA rodeo producer in the 1950s and 1960s. He sold his company to the Elra Beutler and Son producers. In 1980 B. D.'s son, Sammy, carried on the family tradition by forming the Andrews Rodeo Company.

I did not attend the 1993 rodeo. Had I suspected that it would be Ken's last rodeo that he promoted, I'm sure that I would have been there. Instead as a member of the Durant Chamber of Commerce I was co-chairperson of the 1993 Wild West Rodeo Round-Up Days Breakfast in Durant and the top ticket sales person.

No. 15. Ruth, outfitted to co-chair the Durant 1993
Wild West Rodeo Round-up Days & Breakfast.
Photo courtesy of *Denison Herald*.

This was the first year that the PRCA-sanctioned Ada Pro Rodeo was selected for the Dodge Truck Rodeo Series. The winner of the highest total points in the Series at the end of the year would be awarded the use of a new Dodge truck for one year. Chaprell Dodge of Ada was proud to be a part of the Dodge truck promotion.

As usual, Ken engaged top specialty acts. On opening night Leon and Vicki Adams were back to perform with Leon riding his brahmas, "Geronimo" and "Apache," Roman style and Vicki performing with her white horse, "Silverado."

Young trick roper Kyle Lane met the greatest of the legendary trick ropers, J. W. Stoker, when Ken scheduled Stoker for what would be Ken's last rodeo. Stoker starred in the movies, "Bus Stop," with Marilyn Monroe, and in "Bronco Billy," with Clint Eastwood. He performed overseas in the 1970s, 1980s, and 1990s. Stoker won numerous specialty act awards in the United States.

"Ken was a history lesson every time he spoke," Kyle Lane said. "He knew everyone in rodeo, dead or alive."

Although Kyle enjoyed trick roping, he loved training show horses even more. He won three world championships since 2002 at the American Quarter Horse Association, Oklahoma City; the Paint Horse World Title, Fort Worth, Texas; and the Pinto National Championship, Tulsa, Oklahoma.

Jim Bob Feller, PRCA rodeo clown and barrel man, was featured at the 1991 National Finals Rodeo Wrangler Bullfight. He practically brought a zoo with him for his acts: his trick pony Rosco; his duck herding border collie, "Deputy Dawg," and his barrel racing dog, Buddy. Rodeo announcer, Don Endsley, played the straight man in all of Feller's acts, especially the one with his bucking 1923 Ford.

Feller was a bull rider and saddle bronc rider in his younger years. He knew it was just as important for the clown to study the bulls and know their behavior as it was for the bull rider. The bull fighter clown must distract the bull from the cowboy when he hit the ground but he must also protect himself. Feller made it safely into his specially lined barrel every time. Bull fighter clowns bring their own barrels and have them padded inside.

Because announcer, Don Endsley, returned frequently to the Ada Pro Rodeo he became known as the "Voice" of the Ada Pro Rodeo. He announced with Tom Hadley in the 1970s, several times in the 1980s, and the last three rodeos Ken promoted in the 1990s. His voice was often heard on Wrangler TV commercials and the Dodge truck rodeo ads. Don Endsley announced nearly 200 rodeos a year and the National Rodeo Finals, Denver National Western, Texas Finals, Houston Livestock Show, Dodge City Round-Up and many others during his career.

The Andrews Company brought their champion livestock. Sammy Andrews from Addielou, Texas, brought Skoal's Outlaw Willie, the 1991 PRCA Bucking Bull of the Year. This was Andrews' first top stock award.

Ken booked the old time country entertainers, Billy Joe Royal and Johnny Rodriguez, and young musicians,

Tracy Byrd and Doug Supernaw who were climbing the charts. The Fast Lane South band played every night.

Tracy Byrd from Vidor, Texas, played opening night, August 4. His first single, "That's the Thing About a Memory," was popular with radio audiences. His second single, "Someone to Give My Love To," was a former hit by Johnny Paycheck and it gave Byrd attention nationwide. Byrd played with the Mark Chesnutt band before he formed his own band. Naturally, his fans were called, "Byrd Watchers."

Billy Joe Royal entertained Thursday, August 5. His career spanned three decades like Ken's. He sang pop, country, rhythm and blues. Among his hit singles were, "I'll Pin a Note on Your Pillow," "It Keeps Right on Hurtin'," and "Tell It Like It Is." "Boondocks," written by Joe South, brought him national attention. Recent hits were "Burned Like a Rocket" and "Out of Sight and On My Mind." He appeared on Dick Clark's "Cavalcade of Stars."

Johnny Rodriguez returned August 6. He played at the rodeo and dance in the 1970s. His debut album, titled, "Introducing Johnny Rodriguez," was number one on the charts. He wrote fifteen number one hits, starting with, "You Always Come Back to Hurting Me." He won the "Trendsetter Award for the first Mexican-American to capture a national audience and recorded "The Wind Beneath My Wings" in English and Spanish. He received many awards in the United States and Mexico.

In a letter to me Johnny Rodriguez shared his memories of performing at the arena. "The first time I played for Ken and Ruth Lance at their Ken Lance Sports

Arena was in 1974. The weather was perfect that year, but when I returned in 1978, the weather wasn't as good and it was lightning all around. I didn't want to perform in the arena in that kind of weather. Ken got a little upset, but he got over it by the time the dance started. Ken Lance is a great cowboy and easy to work for."[53]

Saturday, August 7, Doug Supernaw shared parade grand marshal honors in downtown Ada with Jimmie Thomas, the 1993 recipient of the Ada Western Heritage Award of Merit. Supernaw was the featured entertainer at the rodeo and dance. He was on the road on his first national tour but he had been writing songs since high school. In 1987 Supernaw was a staff songwriter in Nashville with a Music City publishing company. He returned to Texas, formed his own band, "Texas Steel," and released his debut album, "Red and Rio Grande."

Sheryl Hannigan, 1993 Miss Rodeo America, rode in the grand entry. Among her many accomplishments were awards won in barrel racing, cutting horse competitions, and quarter horse shows. She was a senior at California Polytechnic State University in San Luis Obispo, California.

Miss Rodeo Oklahoma, Lucynda Hendricks, from Ketchum, Oklahoma, rode in the parade Saturday. She earned her bachelor's degree in psychology and was working on her master's degree in marriage and family therapy. She planned to operate a horse ranch as part of her work as a family counselor.

In the Miss Rodeo Oklahoma Pageant, she won in horsemanship, speech, and interview. Her co-contestants

145

also voted her Miss Congeniality. Ken received a thank you note from Lucynda saying, "You really know how to entertain the public."[54]

The computer age had arrived but Ken never had time to purchase one and learn how to use it. Lori Andrews brought along a computer and programmed the rodeo data on it for Ken. It was a big help. After the rodeo, Ken accepted Charles Holbrook's invitation to take a much needed vacation and travel with him to Australia. Ken came back refreshed and ready to plan for the next year.

In 1994 the dance club was temporarily closed for renovations and reopened in the spring. Unfortunately, Ken was financially unable to promote a rodeo anymore. He had used up all his credit. Many old friends had moved away. It was harder to recruit enough dependable help at rodeo time.

The entertainers had raised their prices and required larger advance payments. In the early days we paid the entertainers after the dance when we counted the money on the kitchen table. We never seemed to be able to get ahead and maintain a savings account to fall back on in hard times. It was always hard times.

Jim Shoulders said that Ken's biggest problem was that he had too many friends. Ken would loan his last dollar to a friend in need, knowing it probably would not be paid back. He always set aside free rodeo tickets for family and friends and the kids down the road. Others managed to slip in free without tickets. I was surprised at the number of adults who later admitted to me that when they were kids they would sneak in free to see the rodeo.

In 1994 Ken reined in his dream of thirty years. Instead of a rodeo in the arena in August, there would be a Ken Lance Tribute in October. In a downtown ceremony Ada mayor, Barbara Young, proclaimed October 17-22, 1994, as Ken Lance Appreciation Week. A parade marched through town on Saturday, October 22, just like it always did on the final day of the rodeo.

I was there, accompanied by June's daughter, Tanya Proctor Simmons, and her friend, Lisa Simmons. Ken was glad to see Tanya again. She represented a happier time in 1964, when Ken and I baby-sat Tanya and her three brothers, Mike, Terry, and Ricky, for three weeks while the arena was being built.

The previous week, on October 15, the McEntire family was honored at the second annual McSwain Music Theater Country Music Awards with the "Mae Axton" award. The McEntires had been a part of our lives through all the years of the Ken Lance Sports Arena operation.

Reba no longer performed in dance clubs because the cigarette smoke was too damaging to her throat and lungs. Instead she pursued a highly successful career in concerts, movies, a TV series of her own, and a run on Broadway starring as Annie Oakley. Reba would always be cherished by her Ada Pro Rodeo fans who still danced to the fiddling and singing of her brother, Pake McEntire.

On the day of the Tribute to Ken Lance, eighteen-year-old Oklahoman, Blake Shelton, was featured in a concert in the arena. He moved from Ada to Nashville

147

after he appeared on stage in Nashville in the spring. Larry Large, our former house band leader of the Country Lancers, had joined Shelton's band.

Larry said that Ken always was a good judge of talent in the entertainment and rodeo business. Apparently Larry was a good judge of talent, too, when he signed on with Blake Shelton. Larry's wife, Carol, was president of the Blake Shelton Fan Club.[55]

There were awards, specialty acts, and a calf scramble. The Chickasaw Spirit Riders rode in on their horses racing through the criss-cross, pass-through, and wagon wheel routines, and the feather display. The Chickasaw Dance Troupe performed traditional dances in colorful costumes.

Ken was glad to see his longtime friend, trick roper, George Taylor, who performed with his palomino paint horse, Mego. George recalled that he saw Ken and Ken's sister, Junie, at a Konawa parade when George was a child. Later he saw his first rodeo at the Ken Lance Sports Arena and fell in love with the rodeo life.

George Taylor tried bareback bronc riding, calf roping, clowning, bulldogging, trick roping, roman riding, and training the animals he would need in his act. In other words, he did it all. Ken looked forward to George's phone call every fourth of July thanking Ken for inspiring him.

The Chickasaw Industries, Ltd. sponsored the bull riding event at the Tribute. Billy Downard, owner of the Mile High Bull Company, provided the bucking bulls. In retirement Ken would serve as a committee member for the Chickasaw Bullfights and the All-Indian Rodeo.

In keeping with the spirit of the Tribute, I wore a tan western dress with tan fringe and matching tan western hat, accented with chocolate brown Justin boots and the trophy belt buckle Ken gave me years earlier.

The buckle was embossed with the words, "All Around Cowgirl, Ken Lance Sports Arena, Ruth Lance." When Ken gave it to me I said, "Ken, I'm not an all around cowgirl." But Ken's idea of his all around cowgirl was his partner who worked behind the scenes. Ken replied, "I can put you in any department and you can do it. You can do it all." He trained me. He should know.

No. 16 Tanya Proctor Simmons with her Uncle Ken and Aunt Ruth at the Tribute to Ken, October, 1994. Family photo.

Ken was never heard to say, "I don't have a thing to wear." He changed clothes several times a day according to the activity on the schedule. His countless western shirts and Wrangler jeans were always pressed perfectly at the cleaners. His dozens of pairs of boots were always highly polished. As for his hats, I lost count.

He gave away his shirts to his admirers. He gave monogrammed shirts to trick roper, Kyle Lane, "because we have the same initials." Another time he told Guy Milner, a fellow committee member on the Revenge of the Bulls event, to choose one of three shirts Ken thought would look good on him. While Guy was trying to decide which shirt to choose, Ken solved his problem. "Oh, go ahead and take all three," he grinned.

Ken and I often wore matching shirts. Therefore, I changed clothes after the Tribute parade and wore one of our matching shirts, a red, white, and blue western one, for the evening. The next morning, when Tanya and I joined the others for breakfast at the Holiday Inn, I wore a blue denim dress with silver trim and silver buttons and my blue Justin boots.

It had been a tearful, bittersweet ending to a career Ken and I once shared with each other and with our dads. I'm glad I didn't know that Ken was losing the arena and his home to the bank. Tanya and I thought he was retiring. In a letter to my sister, June, I poured out my heart:

"The citizens of Ada and Pontotoc County rolled out the red carpet to Ken for his retirement. It was a day Tanya and I will never forget. We were so proud for Ken. People did appreciate what he had done for the community. Inside the Ken Lance Sports Arena I said a quiet prayer to God as I looked around the arena.

"Lord, because Daddy believed in Ken's ability, he enabled Ken to help so many people in promoting their careers, plus look at the jobs he gave local people for the thirty-four years that Ken was at the helm of the Ken Lance Sports Arena. Thank you, God. Amen."

The tears rolled down my cheeks as I sat on the empty bleachers, and my mind wandered back to the beginning, the exciting year of 1964.[56]

No. 17. An eager crowd awaits the next event at the Ken Lance Sports Arena. Photo by Rhonda Hulsey.

151

CHAPTER V.

Epilogue: The End of an Era

In October, 1994, a citation, bearing the seal of the State of Oklahoma House of Representatives, was read and presented to Ken as follows:

> Whereas, Ken Lance will be saluted in a special Oklahoma tribute at the Ken Lance Sports Arena in Ada, Oklahoma, on Saturday, October 22, 1994:
>> and
>
> Whereas, the week of October17-22, 1994, has been proclaimed a period in state history to pay special tribute to Ken Lance, who has kept alive Oklahoma's great cowboy heritage for the past thirty-four years;
>> and
>
> Whereas, the Oklahoma House of Representatives is pleased to join with friends, family, and the music, and rodeo industry in honoring a cowboy legend,
>> Ken Lance,
>
> Now, therefore, pursuant to the motion of Representative Danny Hilliard and Representative Jim Dunegan the Oklahoma House of Representatives extends to Ken Lance sincere congratulations and directs that this citation be presented.

The citation was signed by Representative Danny Hilliard, Representative Jim Dunegan, and Speaker Glen D. Johnson.

The words, "state history," and "cowboy legend,"stood out to me in the citation honoring Ken. In Oklahoma's history, he had truly become a cowboy legend. His was not a "rags to riches" story but a dream fulfilled. For me, the Ken Lance Sports Arena show place was my baby but for Ken it was his vision of a lifetime. Babies grow up and leave home, but visions glow and fade into someone else's dream.

Former state Representative, Jim Dunegan, wrote to June and me in 2006 about his recollections:

"Ken and Ruth always had a first class rodeo, professional cowboys and cowgirls, plus outstanding country and western entertainers. I feel honored to have been associated with Ken and Ruth Lance throughout the years and appreciate the opportunities they have given young people in the rodeo and entertainment industry.[1]

The "cowboy legend" was further endorsed the following spring, April 18, 1995, when the Ada Area Chamber of Commerce honored Ken with the chairman's "Living Legend Award." Chickasaw Governor Bill Anoatubby made the presentation. Although Ken had retired from producing rodeos in the Ken Lance Sports Arena, he had not retired from the rodeo culture. Ken supported the All-Indian rodeos.

In May, Ken offered his years of experience and talent in promotion to the enterprises of the Chickasaw Nation. Stanley Foster, chairman of the Revenge of the

Bull committee, welcomed Ken as a committee member. He said that everything he learned about promotion he learned from Ken.

Many of Ken's old friends now participated in the annual "Revenge of the Bulls" bull riding event in Ada at the Pontotoc County Agri-Plex. Jim Shoulders was still signing autographs and inspiring young bull riders.

No. 18. Ken and Jim Shoulders talk about the good old days.

Agent Ray Bingham still booked specialty acts like he did for so many years for events at the Ken Lance Sports Arena. Bull fighter clown, Lecile Harris, was still in tip top shape with his wit delighting the audience and his crazy maneuvers frustrating the bulls. Gene Watson was still making hearts throb with his own style of singing.

In 1998 Ken was inducted into the Chickasaw Nation Hall of Fame in Tishomingo. He worked at the gift shop in the Carl Albert Health Facility in Ada and was proud to earn his 10-year pin in 2006 as Director of Volunteers in the gift shop.

"Lance was loved by all his volunteers," said Chickasaw Legislator Mary Jo Green. "He was too generous for his own good, sometimes giving his last dollar to someone needing gas to get home."[2]

Chickasaw Governor Bill Anoatubby wrote to the authors on May 1, 2006:

"Mr. Lance is a wonderful asset to the Chickasaw Nation as well as to the world of rodeo. Ken Lance's contributions to rodeo are countless. He helped to make rodeoing one of the most respected and highly attended events in this part of the country. Ken's easygoing, polite manner makes him easy to work with, yet his tenacity ensures that whatever goal he sets, he attains. His leadership and genuine love of the rodeo and the competition between cowboys in their sports, and between cowgirls in their sports, certainly contributed to the popularity of the rodeos he put together.

"The Chickasaw nation is certainly fortunate to count Ken Lance among our own. He brings the same devotion that he has for rodeoing to his work with our people. We all benefit from Ken Lance and believe that his accomplishments will never be forgotten."[3]

Chief Gregory E. Pyle, chief of the Choctaw Nation of Oklahoma, also was pleased that my sister and I were writing Ken's stories for posterity.

"The Ken Lance Arena is a well-known landmark for people who love country music, and the recognition your book will offer is certainly deserved. Cowboys, entertainers, and those of us who just love music will all be sure to enjoy reading your stories of events held at the arena. Rodeo heritage is an important part of the history of our great state and I will be proud to see the memories live on."[4]

A dozen of Ken's friends helped him to move out of the home in which he had lived for so many years. He moved across the road into the trailer where his dad had lived before he died and where his brother, George, was living when George died. Ken simply couldn't leave the land where his dream had been born and nurtured.

He said, "It started from humble beginnings and it returned to an humble ending. We lost the arena. I did. Sometimes it kinda breaks my heart but I learned a lot."[5]

Although people spoke of him as a living legend, Ken said that he didn't feel like a legend but he felt as old as one. Several things happened to lift his spirits. The road on which the arena complex was located was renamed, "Ken Lance Road."

No. 19. Tanya Proctor Simmons awaits her Uncle Ken's covered wagon on Ken Lance Sports Arena Road. Family photo.

The dance club was featured in the section on "Clubs with Stayin' Power," in the 1995 book, *Honky-Tonks: A Guide to Country Dancin' and Romancin'* by Eileen Sisk. In 2004 K. Deek Moore recorded a song titled, "Cinch (Devil's Juice)," about a conservation between champion bull rider, Charlie Sampson, and Cinch at the Ken Lance Rodeo.[6]

Ken was a family man and a marrying man. He couldn't let go of his wives. When a divorce was final, he either remarried the same woman, or kept in touch and married another. His marriage to Lola June ended in divorce again. Her dogs followed him home. The dogs didn't understand that they did not have custody of Ken. Lola June died a short time later.

Ken met his next and last wife, Malinda LaVey Clifton, at a barrel racing event. Ever the gentleman, Ken asked a friend to introduce him to the attractive woman sitting with three equally attractive young ladies, who happened to be her daughters, Kim, Stacey, and Casey. They had come to watch Malinda's (she preferred to be called Linda) granddaughter compete in the barrel racing event.

A few days later Ken drove up to Linda's rural home in his white Cadillac. She couldn't believe it was Ken. Her daughters were delighted. He had fallen in love with their mother, and they had fallen for him. Ken and Linda were married, December 3, 1994, in Las Vegas, Nevada. Unexpectedly, Linda died May 5, 2005. Ken comforted her daughters and their families in their shared grief.

Linda's youngest daughter, Casey Thomas, and her husband Trevor, purchased Ken's old home place, next to the arena complex. Ken was overjoyed. The home had come back into the family at last.

Casey and Trevor's sons, seven-year-old Kaleb and five-year-old Kash, liked to ride with Ken on the golf cart. Back in the 1960s, my nephews called it the "ranch buggy." Of course the old golf cart had been replaced many times through the years.

In the meantime, my husband, Dr. John Krattiger, died, February 15, 2000. On December 28, 2001, I married Dr. Truman Wester from Denison, Texas. Truman's wife had also died recently. Truman and John were life long friends from their graduate student days at the University of Oklahoma.

Truman became president of Grayson County College, Denison, Texas, where he retired as President Emeritus in 1982. Both John and Truman were most supportive of June's and my commitment to write the history of the Ken Lance Sports Arena. Coincidentally, Truman's uncle, Ada contractor Simpson "Simp" Moore, had constructed the wooden Ferdinand the Bull for the Ada Rodeo before the days of the Ken Lance Sports Arena. Truman and I have the original wooden horns today.

On Wednesday, September 20, 2006, Ken left work early at the Carl Albert Indian Health Facility. He couldn't seem to shake the flu-like symptoms he had been suffering for more than a week. Several friends phoned him that night and reported that he thought he had bronchitis. Casey brought a warm supper to him. The next morning she phoned but there was no answer. Casey and Trevor went over to Ken's trailer and knocked on the door. No reply. They went inside and found him dead in his bed.

Truman and I were at home in Denison, Texas. My sister, June, was downstairs at the computer, editing the manuscript for this book. She asked me to call Ken to check on some details. But there was no answer at his home and he had not shown up for work yet when I called the health facility.

Then Ken's stepdaughter, Kim Ward, phoned. When she started talking, I started screaming. Tears flooded my eyes and I stumbled down the stairs with Truman right behind me. "Ken's dead!" I shrieked as I shoved the phone into June's hand. Truman and I clung to each other in disbelief.

Kim told June that Ken said they should call Ruth if anything happened to him. "Ruthie will know what to do." Others called with the same message. Ken's sister, Junie DeVaughan, his niece, Sandi Sanders, Tom Criswell, funeral director at Criswell Funeral Home. They all said, "Ruthie will know what to do."

Ken put a lot of faith in me and I set to work to carry out his wishes as he had instructed me to do.

"We're on our own now," June said. "We owe it to Ken to see this book through to publication." It was as though Ken were writing his own epilogue and we were transcribing it.

Ken died on Thursday, September 21, 2006, the morning before the autumn equinox. Somehow that seemed significant to his Chickasaw heritage. Many friends visited with the family at Criswell Funeral Home in Ada throughout the weekend. They swapped stories before Ken's open casket, as though he might chuckle and join in the storytelling himself.

The women made sure that Ken's snow white hair was combed the way he always combed it. "Ken was very particular about his hair," a Chickasaw volunteer said.

Over 1000 people gathered to mourn his death at the funeral, September 25, 2006, at Evangelistic Temple, Ada. Preceding the service, the church membership provided the meal for the family in the church's dining hall. Carl Albert Indian Health Facility prepared the meats.

In the sanctuary, recordings of Ken's favorite cowboy songs played softly as mourners were ushered to the pews. Countless flower arrangements flanked the open casket. Ken wore a bright blue shirt with mounted cowboys silhouetted on its border.

In the midst of the cascade of flowers on the casket, stood a pair of Ken's black boots, his black western hat, and his trusty lariat. On the floor stood a pair of brown cowboy boots holding wild flowers. The gift card bore the names of his step-grandsons, Kaleb and Kash Thomas, the children of Casey and Trevor.

The flag of the Chickasaw Nation stood to the right of the casket. An easel holding a gold-framed painting of Ken and his dad team roping was placed to the left of the casket. Appropriately, two saddles and lariats rested on saddle stands at either end of the podium, symbolizing the lifelong partnership and mutual love of roping shared by father and son.

Reverend Randall Christy, pastor of Union Valley Baptist Church, officiated. "The cowboy is the symbol of freedom," he said. "I'll always remember Ken riding out in the arena with that huge American flag, celebrating the great freedom we enjoy in this country."

No. 20. Old Glory waves high as Ken rides carrying our nation's flag. Photo by Louise Hoehman.

Pat Turner, who devoted himself to chauffeuring Ken on trips in his later years and checking on him every weekend, presided over the eulogy and storytelling by other friends of Ken.

We laughed. We cried. We clapped along with Pake McEntire's fiddling when he played, "The Orange Blossom Express." Pake played and sang a sentimental medley of western songs Ken loved to hear him play at the rodeos and dances.

Jeannie Coplin, wearing her volunteer's smock from the Carl Albert Health Facility, rose and said, "I speak on behalf of the volunteers. We loved Ken and Ken loved us and spoiled us. Corman Sharp was ninety years old and Ken spoiled her rotten. She loved Ken and Ken loved her." The volunteers sat as a group in reserved seats at the funeral. One lady came in her wheelchair.

Bob Macy's son, Brett, represented his father since Bob was recovering from back surgery and was unable to attend. Bob and Ken, close friends for more than forty years, had promised to be pall bearers at each other's funeral for whoever died first. Brett said, "Since Dad couldn't fulfill that promise, the score remains a tie."

Then Brett escorted me to the podium. I read the inscription on a photo Reba gave to Ken and me back in 1982:

"Thanks for all the years of love, faith, and music. And thanks for introducing me to Red. That started all of this. Reckon I'll ever regret it? I seriously doubt that. But again, we love you all and may God bless you both forever! Love, Reba."[63]

She also e-mailed her condolences to me in response to my notifying her of Ken's death.

"Thanks so much for letting us know about Ken. I'm in Los Angeles and won't be able to make it to the funeral. I just hope you know how much you and Ken always meant to me and my family. There's no telling where Pake, Susie, and my careers would be today if it hadn't been for you two. Always, Reba."[64]

Susie McEntire Luchsinger was performing in Grand Junction, Colorado, the day of the funeral. Even so, she e-mailed me at 1:37 a.m. after the show was over.

"I know that Ken would have understood that the show must go on. Please give my regrets to all the family. In Christ, Susie Luchsinger."[65]

Back in the 1970s when Loretta Lynn's Pow-Wow couldn't get the Stomp Dancers from the McAlester prison anymore because some of the trustees would escape, Ken suggested the Singing McEntires. We could always count on them to come through, with one, two, and sometimes three McEntires on stage.

Jim Shoulders, pall bearer, said that Ken was probably trying to start another rodeo up yonder. He didn't know how true that was until Reverend Christy made a surprising announcement.

The Ken Lance Sports Arena had been purchased and would be reopened as the 3 Crosses Cowboy Church, Kids Rodeo Camp, and Ken Lance Sports Arena. The dance pavilion would be renovated and re-opened as the 3 Crosses Cowboy Church. The arena would be used for kids' rodeo camp, and the complex would be made available for community events.[66]

Ken and Linda rededicated their lives to Christ at a Cowboys Church worship service at Bob Byrd's ranch a couple of years before Linda's death. Reverend Christy was present that night.

At the close of the funeral service, a video of Ken's life was shown. Music played softly. Many people in the audience were pictured with Ken at happier times.

The last frame pictured Ken, mounted on his horse, ready to depart. As the picture faded, we heard the tune, "The Cowboy Rides Away."

No. 21. "Great Ride, Ken. See You at the Next Go Round." Cowboys' farewell message. Photo courtesy of *Ada Evening News.*

The funeral procession, led by police escort, was directed past the Ken Lance Sports Arena for a last nostalgic look at the place where thousands had captured exciting memories, cheering for cowboys and cowgirls, dancing to live music of country western entertainers of a bygone era. The procession continued a few miles farther to Highland Cemetery, Stonewall, Oklahoma, for the grave side service.

On October 20-21, 2006, exactly twelve years after the Chickasaw Enterprises sponsored the bull riding event at the Tribute for Ken in the Ken Lance Sports Arena, they dedicated the Revenge of the Bulls world championship rodeo bullfight finals and concert "in loving memory of Ken Lance."[67]

They say old soldiers never die, they just fade away. Old cowboys never die either. They just ride off into the sunset. As Ken rode off into eternity, it was comforting to know that his cowboy legacy would live on in his "watermelon patch," now a historic site where future generations would learn to rope and ride their cowboy and cowgirl dreams in the twenty-first century.

END NOTES

INTRODUCTION

1. Gail Hughbanks Woerner, *Cowboy Up: The History of Bull Riding*, p. 158.
2. Martha Josey, personal letter to Ruth Lance Wester, September 11, 2006.
3. Gail Hughbanks Woerner, "Buck Steiner: A Legend," p. 34-35.
4. Reba McEntire with Tom Carter, *Reba: My Story*, p. 54.

CHAPTER I. Ropin' the Dream in the 1960s

5. Ken Lance, "Cowpoke Gossip from Oklahoma and Texas," *Hoofs and Horns,* August 1951, p. 16.
6. The Dawes General Allotment Act, passed February 8, 1887, allocated reservation land to be distributed to individual members of a tribe. Head of household was eligible to receive 160 acres. Unmarried adults received 80 acres.
7. Doug Williams, rodeo announcer, letter to Ruth Lance Wester, August, 2006.
8. Bob Byrd, rodeo clown, interview with author, Ruth Lance Wester, August 12, 2006.
9. The Girls Rodeo Association (GRA) was organized with thirty-eight members, February 28, 1948, at San Angelo, Texas (see *Hoofs and Horns*, May, 1948, p. 24). In 1967 the Rodeo Cowboys Association board (RCA) voted to include the GRA barrel racing contest at the National Rodeo Finals. Previously, the GRA finalists came from the All Girl Rodeos. Mary Lou LeCompte, *Cowgirls of the Rodeo: Pioneer Professional Athletes* (Urbana and Chicago: University of Illinois Press, 1993. Illini Books, baberback edition, 2000): p. 177

10. George O. Carney, "From Lee to Reba and Beyond: Oklahoma Women in American Popular Music," *The Chronicles of Oklahoma,* 79 (3 Fall, 2001): p. 260-277.
11. Linda Bolen, phone interview with author, Ruth Lance Wester, September 20, 2006.
12. Martha (Arthur) Josey qualified for the National Finals Rodeo in four decades: 1968, 1969, 1978 to 1981, 1985, 1987, 1988, and 1990. She was awarded a medal in the 1988 Winter Olympics in Calgary, Canada. Today she and her husband, R.E. Josey, Texas Cowboy Hall of Fame honoree, host professional rodeo clinics and schools in world champion barrel racing, horsemanship, and calf roping at the Josey Ranch, Marshall, Texas.
13. Martha (Arthur) Josey, letter to Ruth Lance Wester, September 11, 2006.
14. Jan Storey, letter to Ruth Lance Wester, September 2006.
15. Contract between Ken Lance and Willie Nelson, September 28, 1967, for a performance scheduled for November 16,1967, through Alamo Production: American Federation of Musicians of the United States & Canada, Local No. 257.

CHAPTER III. Thrilling the Crowds in the 1970s

16. Jan Storey, IRA rodeo announcer, letter to Ruth Lance Wester, August, 2006.
17. Larry Large, Country Lancers band leader, e-mail to Ruth Lance Wester, October 25, 2006.
18. Kenny Seratt, letter to Ruth Lance Wester, October 31, 2005, and e-mail, November 3, 2005.
19. Larry Large, Country Lancers bandleader, e-mail to Ruth Lance Wester, October 25, 2006.
20. In 1991 Red Steagall was voted Official Cowboy Poet of Texas by the state legislature. Read his poetry and stories

in his books: *The Fence That Me and Shorty Built; Born to This Land; Cowboy Corner Conversations.* See bibliography.

21. Barbara Mandrell with George Vecsey, *Get to the Heart: My Story,* New York: Bantam Books, 1990.
22. Loudilla Johnson, letter to editor," Country Music News, August 14, 1972.
23. "CMN Visit Loretta Lynn Pow-Wow in Ada," *Country Music News*, August 14, 1972.
24. Ray Bingham, e-mail to Ruth Lance Wester, April 24, 2006. "Billy Parker said Ken gave him the inspiration he needed to go on with his career, when he was starting out on his own. Said he will forever be grateful to Ken."
25. *Rodeo News,* July 1973, p. 12.
26. For more information Clem McSpadden's contributions to Oklahoma's rodeo history, see, "Clem McSpadden, 'Old Gravel Voice Guy,' Still Announcing," by Norman Edward Rourke, *The Ketchpen,* Volume XV, p. 27-30.
27. Jackie McEntire, letter to Ruth Lance Wester, December 4, 2005.
28. Reba McEntire, letter to Ruth Lance Wester, November 4, 2005.
29. See note 27.
30. Red Steagall, e-mail to Ruth Lance Wester, November 4, 2005.
31. "Living Honorees," *The Ketchpen,* Volume XVII, Number 1, p. 21.
32. Melinda (Pierce) Johnson, letter to Ruth Lance Wester, December 13, 2006.
33. Larry and Carol Large, e-mail to Ruth Lance Wester, October 25, 2006. Larry also told this story at Ken's funeral, September 29, 2006.
34. Reba McEntire, e-mail to Ruth Lance Wester, January 4, 2006.

35. "The Cowboy from Hogshooter Creek," by Judy Goodspeed, *The Ketchpen*, Volume XVII, Number 1, Spring, 2005. p. 709.

CHAPTER III. Bulldogging the 1980s

36. Ray Bingham, entertainers' agent, e-mail to Ruth Lance Wester, April 24, 2007.
37. Reba McEntire, letter to Ken Lance, December 18, 1980.
38. Kristine Fredriksson, *American Rodeo, From Buffalo to Big Business.* p. 196-197.
39. Terri Larney, letter to Ruth Lance Wester, October 30, 2006.
40. June Proctor, *The Night the Angels Cried: A Mother's True Story,* 2003. Self-published with Morris Publishing Company. Available direct from author at 18921 FM 1497, Paris, Texas, 75462. $9.95 plus $3.00 shipping and handling. Texas residents add 8.25% sales tax.
41. Pake McEntire, letter to Ruth Lance Wester, January 5, 2005.
42. Glen Hyden, *Ada Evening News,* August 5, 1983.
43. "Rodeo Gives Business a Shot in the Arm Here," by Glen Hyden, *Ada Evening News*, August 3, 1983.
44. *Pro Rodeo Sports News,* 1975; *Rodeo in America: Wranglers, Roughstock, and Paydirt,"* by Wayne S. Wooden and Gavin Ehringer.
45. Susie (McEntire) Luchsinger, e-mail to Ruth Lance Wester, January 11, 2006.
46. Paul and Susie Luchsinger, *A Tender Road Home,* p. 148-149.
47. "Hey, Ken, It's Rodeo Time," editorial, *The Ada Times,* p. 3, August 5, 1989.

End Notes

CHAPTER. IV. Reining in the Dream in the 1990s

48. *Cowboy Up: The History of Bull Riding* by Gail Hughbanks Woerner. P. 246-247.
49. Editorial, *Ada Evening News,* August 6, 1990.
50. Interview with Kyle Lane at Ada, Oklahoma, by June Proctor, co-author, September 22, 2006.
51. "Dea Lance Loved Roping and Rodeo," by Tony Pippen, staff writer, *Ada Evening News,* Tuesday, November 26, 1991.
52. Pam Williams Queen, e-mail to Ruth Lance Wester, August 21, 2006.
53. Johnny Rodriguez, letter to Ruth Lance Wester, September, 2006.
54. Miss Rodeo Oklahoma, Lucynda Hendricks, letter to Ken Lance, August 24, 1993.
55. Larry Large, e-mail to Ruth Lance Wester, October 25, 2006.
56. Ruth Lance Krattiger, letter to June Proctor, May, 1996.

CHAPTER V. Epilogue: The End of an Era

57. Former Oklahoma Representative Jim Dunegan, letter to Ruth Lance Wester and June Proctor, 2006.
58. "Local Rodeo Icon Dies," by Liz Brewer, staff writer, *Ada Evening News,* September 22, 2006.
59. Chickasaw Nation Governor Bill Anoatubby, letter to the authors, May, 2006.
60. Chief Gregory E. Pyle, Choctaw Nation of Oklahoma, letter to Ruth Lance Wester, September 5, 2006.
61. Ken Lance and Ruth Lance Wester in videotaped interview by Film Works, LLC, October 2001.
62. *Honky-Tonks: Guide to Country Dancin' and Romancin.'* by Eileen Sisk. p. 96-99; Deek Moore, 31 Album, produced by Dan Vogel for Room Indigo Productions, Austin, Texas.

63. Reba McEntire, e-mail to Ruth Lance Wester, April 17, 1982.
64. Reba McEntire, e-mail to Ruth Lance Wester,
    September 22, 2006.
65. Susie McEntire Luchsinger, e-mail to Ruth Lance Wester,
    September 26, 2007.
66. Tax-exempt donations can be made to 3 Crosses Cowboy
    Church, c/o The Gospel Station Network, P.O. Box 1343,
    Ada, Oklahoma 78420. Phone 1-800-557-8815.
    www.thegospelstation.com.
67. Stanley Foster still chaired the Revenge of the Bulls
    committee. Members serving at the time of Ken's death were:
    Guy Milner, Tony Mooney, Dana Johnson, Leslie Rogers,
    Deanna Townsend, Jerry Deatherage, Jimmy James, Brian
    England, Carol Snyder, and Andrew Wade.

BIBLIOGRAPHY

Books:

Allen, Michael. *Rodeo Cowboys in the North American Imagination.* Reno and Las Vegas: University of Nevada Press, 1998.

Beals, Imogene. *Boots and Saddles.* Siloam Springs, Arkansas: Siloam Springs, Arkansas, 1994.

Fredriksson, Kristine. *American Rodeo: From Buffalo Bill to Big Business.* College Station: Texas A&M University Press, 1985. Second printing, 1993.

Garrison, Walt, with John Tullius. *Once a Cowboy.* New York: Random House, 1988.

Kroeker, Marvin and Guy W. Logsdon, *Ada, Queen City of the Chickasaw Nation: A Pictorial History.* Virginia Beach, Virginia: The Donning Company, 1998.

Lamb, Gene. *Rodeo: Back of the Chutes.* Denver, Colorado: Bell Press, 1956.

Lawrence, Elizabeth Atwood, *Rodeo: An Anthropologist Looks at the Wild and Tame.* Chicago: University of Chicago Press, 1984.

_____ *Hoofbeats and Society: Studies of Human Horse Interaction.* Bloomington: Indiana University Press, 1993.

LeCompte, Mary Lou. *Cowgirls of the Rodeo: Pioneer Professional Athletes.* Urbana and Chicago: University of Illinois Press, 1993. Illini Books paperback edition, 2000.

Luchsinger, Paul & Susie. *A Tender Road Home.* Nashville, Tennessee: Broadman & Holman Publishers, 1997.

173

Bibliography

Mandrell, Barbara with George Vecsey. *Get to the Heart: My Story.* New York: Bantam Books. Hardcover 1990. Paperback 1991.

McCall, Michael. *Country Music Superstars.* New York: BDD Illustrated Books, 1993.

McEntire, Reba.*Comfort from a Country Quilt: Finding New Inspiration and Strength from Old-Fashioned Values.* New York: Bantam Books, 1999.

_____ with Tom Carter. *Reba.* New York: Bantam Books, 1994.

Mellis, Allison Fuss. *Riding Buffaloes and Broncos: Rodeo and Native Traditions in the Northern Great Plains.* Norman, Oklahoma: University of Oklahoma Press, 2003.

Pointer, Larry. *Rodeo Champions: Eight Memorable Moments of Riding, Wrestling, and Roping.* Albuquerque, New Mexico: University of New Mexico,1985.

Porter, Willard H. *Roping and Riding. Fast Horses and Short Ropes.* New York: A.S. Barnes & Co., 1975.

Savitt,Sam. *Rodeo: Cowboys, Bulls, and Broncs.* Garden City, New York: Doubleday, 1963.

Sisk, Eileen. *Honky-Tonks: Guide to Country Dancin' and Romancin'.* New York: Harper Collins West, 1995.

Slatta, Richard W., *The Cowboy Dictionary.* New York: W. W. Norton Company, 1994.

Simbeck, Rob, editor. *American Music Legends.* Published by Cumberland Records for Cracker Barrel, Old Country Store, 2005.

Steagall, Red, edited by Loretta Fulton. *Cowboy Corner Conversations.* State House Press, McMurry University, Abilene, Texas, 2004.

_____. *The Fence That Me and Shorty Built.* Bunkhouse Press, 2001.

Tinkelman, Murray. *Little Britches Rodeo.* New York: Greenwillow Books, 1985.

Bibliography

Woerner, Gail Hughbanks. *Cowboy Up: The History of Bull Riding*. Austin, Texas: Eakin Press, 2001.

_____.*Fearless Funnymen: The History of the Rodeo Clown*. Austin, Texas: Eakin Press, 1993.

_____. *Belly Full of Bedsprings: The History of Bronc Riding*. Austin, Texas: Eakin Press, 1998.

Wooden, Wayne S. & Gavin Ehringer. *Rodeo in America: Wranglers, Roughstock, & Paydirt*. Lawrence, Kansas: University of Kansas Press,1996.

Newspapers, Magazines, History Chronicles

Ada Evening News, Ada, Oklahoma

Hoof and Horns, May, 1948; August, 1951.

The Ketchpen. Rodeo Historical Society, Oklahoma City, Oklahoma.

Rodeo News- May, 1973; July, 1973; April, 1996; Vol 31, No. 2, 1991.

Western Horseman, 1961. Mansfield, Toots. "Calf Roping." Colorado Springs, Colorado

Carney, George O. "From Lee to Reba and Beyond: Oklahoma Women in American Popular Music." *The Oklahoma Chronicles*. Vol.79 Number 3, Fall, 2001. P. 260-277. The Oklahoma Historical Society, Oklahoma City.

Hoy, Jim."Rodeo in American Film." *Heritage of the Great Plains* 23:2 (1990): 26-32.

PRCA Rodeo Programs

39th Annual Ada Championship Rodeo, August 3-7, 1976
40th Annual Ada Championship Rodeo, August 2-6, 1977
41st Annual Ada Championship Rodeo, August 1-5, 1978
42nd Annual Ada Championship Rodeo, August 1-4, 1979
PRCA ProRodeo Official Rodeo Program, Aug. 3-6, 1983

ABOUT THE AUTHORS

Ruth Lance Wester, former wife and business partner of Ken Lance, served in the U.S. Air Force, as an overseas flight attendant to North Africa and Europe. Upon her honorable discharge she was licensed to practice real estate sales in Florida.

She promoted the Ken Lance Sports Arena in partnership with her husband, Ken Lance, for twenty-five years. She later served as director of sales at the Quality Inn, Durant, Oklahoma, and became a certified senior advisor with Team Financial Concepts. In 2001 she was named Ms. Oklahoma Woman by All American Pageants, Inc.

She is an associate member of the International Rodeo Association and a member of the Rodeo Historical Society. She is an active member in the Oklahoma Writers Federation, Inc., and the Red River Writers Club, Durant, Oklahoma.

Ruth Lance Wester resides in Denison, Texas, with her husband, Dr. Truman Wester, president emeritus of Grayson County College, Denison, Texas.

June Proctor is the author of the award winning book, *The Night the Angels Cried: A Mother's True Story*. It was awarded first place in 2003 by the Press Women of Texas and second place by the National Federation of Press Women.

Articles from her weekly column, "Stay Tuned with June," in the *Bryan County Star*, Durant, Oklahoma, also received awards in 2005 and 2006. A preview of *Ropin' the Dream* was published in the *The Ketchpen*, winter 2006 issue, by the Rodeo Historical Society.

She is a retired director of religious education, certified by the U.S. Army Board of Chaplains. Upon her husband's retirement from the U.S. Army Medical Corps, she was awarded the Outstanding Civilian Service Medal for service to soldiers and their families. She holds a master's degree in American history and a master's degree in religious education.

June Proctor resides with her husband, Brigadier General Richard O. Proctor (retired) at Whispering Oaks Ranch, Paris, Texas.

Ropin' the Dream Order Form

Use this convenient order form to order additional copies of
Ropin' the Dream

Please Print:

Name_____

Address_____

City_____ **State**_____

Zip_____

Phone(_____)_____

___ copies of book @ $16.95 each $_____
Postage and handling @ $3.00 per book $_____
TX residents add 8.25% tax $_____
Total amount enclosed $_____

Make checks payable to: Ruth L. Wester

Send order to: Ruth Lance Wester
1130 West Morton Street • Denison, TX 75020

www.ruthlancewester.com